THE WALK

THE WALK
FIVE ESSENTIAL PRACTICES OF THE CHRISTIAN LIFE

The Walk: Five Essential Practices of the Christian Life

978-1-5018-9118-2 Hardcover with jacket
978-1-5018-9119-9 eBook
978-1-501-89120-5 Large Print

The Walk: DVD
978-1-5018-9123-6

The Walk: Leader Guide
978-1-5018-9121-2
978-1-5018-9122-9 eBook

The Walk: Youth Study
978-1-5018-9130-4
978-1-5018-9131-1 eBook

The Walk: Children's Leader Guide
978-1-5018-9132-8

Also by Adam Hamilton

24 Hours That Changed the World

Christianity and World Religions

Christianity's Family Tree

Confronting the Controversies

Creed

Enough

Faithful

Final Words from the Cross

Forgiveness

Half Truths

John

Leading Beyond the Walls

Love to Stay

Making Sense of the Bible

Moses

Not a Silent Night

Revival

Seeing Gray in a World of Black and White

Selling Swimsuits in the Arctic

Simon Peter

Speaking Well

The Call

The Journey

The Way

Unafraid

Unleashing the Word

When Christians Get It Wrong

Why?

For more information, visit www.AdamHamilton.org

ADAM HAMILTON

Author of *Creed: What Christians Believe and Why*

THE
WALK

FIVE ESSENTIAL PRACTICES
OF THE CHRISTIAN LIFE

Abingdon Press
Nashville

THE WALK:
FIVE ESSENTIAL PRACTICES OF THE CHRISTIAN LIFE

Copyright © 2019 Abingdon Press
All rights reserved.

Library of Congress Control Number:2019951460

978-1-5018-9118-2

19 20 21 22 23 24 25 26 27 28—10 9 8 7 6 5 4 3 2 1
MANUFACTURED IN THE UNITED STATES OF AMERICA

CONTENTS

INTRODUCTION
WALKING WITH GOD

During that day's cool evening breeze, they heard the sound of the LORD God walking in the garden; and the man and his wife hid themselves from the LORD God in the middle of the garden's trees. The LORD God called to the man and said to him, "Where are you?"

Genesis 3:8-9

A year before his untimely death in a car accident in 2003, Mike Yaconelli wrote a book called, *Messy Spirituality: God's Annoying Love for Imperfect People.* The book deeply resonated with me. Yaconelli was honest and frank about his own journey with Christ, and how after more than forty years of being a Christian, his faith was still ...messy. And not only his. He told story after story about people, both those in the Bible and people he had personally known, who found grace through Jesus despite the messiness of their lives.

I wrote this book to be a simple guide for the Christian life written for ordinary people whose faith is sometimes messy. It is written for those who wish to follow Jesus, to experience more of God in their lives, and to grow to become the people God wants them to be. It's based upon four decades of reading, study, practice, and striving to live the Christian life, by a person whose faith is sometimes still messy. In it we'll consider five simple practices that Jesus' followers have always pursued as they sought to walk with him. Jesus himself modeled these practices for us. These five are not an exhaustive list of spiritual disciplines. There are an infinite number of ways we might grow in our walk with God. But these five are foundational, and I would say, essential for most of us. If you make these practices a part of the daily rhythm of your life, you'll find that they will play a key role in helping you grow in your faith and, in turn, that they will become an expression and fruit of your increasing faith.

In Matthew 4, Jesus walked along the shoreline of the Sea of Galilee. He came to Simon Peter and Andrew and gave them this simple invitation: "Come, follow me." A few steps later he called James and John to do the same. Sometime later he saw a tax collector named Matthew and said to him, "Follow me." These followers became known as disciples—ones who follow, learn from, and emulate their master. And "to follow" in Greek is *akoloutheo*, which means to accompany on a journey or to walk with someone down a road.

It is this idea of walking with Jesus that we will lean most heavily upon in this book. It is a simple way of thinking about our Christian life. We are followers of

Jesus. We are seeking to learn from him, to emulate him, to go where he wants us to go, to do what he wants us to do, and to walk on the journey of life with him.

Walking with God

The image of walking with God or God walking with us is found throughout the Bible as a metaphor for the life of faith. As the biblical story begins, God is described as *walking* in the garden of Eden, searching for his children as they hid from him. To be sure, this is an anthropomorphism—ascribing human attributes to God—yet the imagery is beautiful and compelling: God walks in our midst, searches for us, and beckons us to walk with him.

When my daughters were small, we would take walks together and they would hold my hand. I loved these walks. Now I've got a five-year-old granddaughter who likes to take my hand and walk with me. There is something about holding her little hand as we walk together that captures how I see my relationship with God.

I picture God loving me as I love my granddaughter, and reaching out his hand toward me, waiting for me to place my hand in his. There is safety and peace and joy in walking with my hand in his hand. This is what Thomas Dorsey wrote of in his much-loved gospel hymn, "Precious Lord, Take My Hand."

Walking is often used in Scripture as a way of speaking about our life with God. God asked Abram and Sarai to load up their things and walk with God to the Promised

Land. This one act of faith and obedience led to Abraham's and Sarah's greatest adventures and richest blessings. At age ninety-nine, God spoke to Abram once again saying, "I am El Shaddai. *Walk* with me" (Genesis 17:1, emphasis added here and in the following examples).

Moses gave these instructions to Israel: "You must *walk* the precise path that the LORD your God indicates for you so that you will live, and so that things will go well for you" (Deuteronomy 5:33). Later, Moses noted, "The LORD will establish you as his own, a holy nation, just as he swore to you, if you keep the LORD your God's commandments and *walk* in his ways" (Deuteronomy 28:9).

The psalmist cries out, "Teach me your way, LORD, so that I can *walk* in your truth" (Psalm 86:11). Israel's prophets called God's people to "*walk* by the LORD's light" (Isaiah 2:5). Micah famously called God's people to "*walk* humbly with your God" (Micah 6:8).

This image of walking with God is found throughout the New Testament too. The Gospels' portrayal of Jesus calling his disciples to follow and to walk with him is a powerful metaphor for the Christian life. As we've seen, to be a Christian is to answer Jesus' call to follow; in the words of an old hymn, it is to "walk with him and talk with him along life's narrow way." As we follow him we "*walk* in the light" (1 John 1:7 NRSV) Paul tells the Romans that they can "*walk* in newness of life" (Romans 6:4). He also commands the Corinthians to "walk by faith, not by sight" (2 Corinthians 5:7 NRSV) In the Bible's closing book, Jesus tells the Church at Sardis that those who remain faithful "will *walk* with me clothed in white" (Revelation 3:4). And when the City of God finally comes on earth, when Paradise is restored, God once again walks on earth with his people, and the nations walk in the light of the Lamb of God (Revelation 21:22-24).

The Christian spiritual life is a life of walking with Christ in our everyday life.

Out of Shape

A couple of years ago, LaVon and I were visiting our daughter Rebecca in New York. She wanted to go hiking in the Catskill Mountains. Upon arriving we took off on a hike to one of her favorite spots. Not ten minutes into the hike I had to sit down. I was winded and didn't feel I could catch my breath. I was not having a heart attack, I was just terribly out of shape.

Over a thirty-five-year period I had watched my weight slowly increase and my physical health slowly decline. At eighteen, I weighed 175 pounds. The week after Christmas, 2017, I stepped on the scale and I was at 208 pounds—up six pounds just from the year before. In addition, my annual physical revealed that my cholesterol was high. My triglycerides were high. A heart scan revealed plaque in my arteries. I hadn't exercised regularly since college.

I wanted to be able to keep up with my daughter when she wanted to hike. I was determined that I would get in shape. My wife told me about a seven-minute workout app for my phone. I thought, *Surely I can work out seven minutes a day*. So I started with seven minutes. That gradually increased to fourteen minutes, then longer still. I began eating better too. Over the next year I lost much of the weight I'd spent thirty-five years putting on. My resting heart rate dropped, my blood work returned to normal levels, and I felt better. The last time I walked with my twenty-nine-year-old daughter, I needed to slow down a bit for her.

Spiritual health is not dissimilar to our physical health. Without spiritual exercises or practices, we will find it difficult to keep up as Christ calls us to follow. We become spiritually lethargic and out of shape. We stray from God's path. Temptation is harder to resist. We don't evidence the fruit of the Spirit. We may exhibit less patience, kindness, mercy, and love. God may seem more distant, and our faith more perfunctory. We worry more as we trust God less. Our thoughts revolve more around ourselves. Our values and priorities shift away from the things God values and prioritizes for us.

Even the earliest Christians struggled with this. In Revelation 2:4-5, Jesus speaks to the Christians at Ephesus, a church founded by Paul and, according to tradition, later shepherded by the apostle John: "I have this against you," Jesus says. "You have let go of the love you had at first. So remember the high point from which you have fallen. Change your hearts and lives and do the things you did at first" (Revelation 2:4-5).

In this little book we'll explore five essential spiritual practices—I think of them like the exercises in my seven-minute workout app: worship and prayer, study, serving, giving, and sharing. For each we'll consider simple ways to get started as well as some concrete goals (I'll invite you to use your hands and fingers as reminders of each practice and the goals). As my physical health increased using the short workout on my phone, I extended my workouts and increased my goals. The same will happen with your pursuit of these spiritual exercises. Here's what I can promise: when pursued daily, these practices will increase your spiritual health, deepen your faith, make you more aware of God's presence, and help you live the Christian life.

With this in mind, let's explore the five essential practices.

CHAPTER 1

WORSHIP AND PRAYER

WORSHIP AND PRAYER
A LIVING HALLELUJAH

O come, let us sing to the LORD;
    let us make a joyful noise to the rock of our
    salvation!
Let us come into his presence with thanksgiving;
    let us make a joyful noise to him with songs of
    praise!
For the LORD is a great God,
    and a great King above all gods.
In his hand are the depths of the earth;
    the heights of the mountains are his also.
The sea is his, for he made it,
    and the dry land, which his hands have
    formed.

O come, let us worship and bow down,
    let us kneel before the LORD, our Maker!
For he is our God,

> and we are the people of his pasture,
> and the sheep of his hand.
>
> *(Psalm 95:1-7, NRSV)*

I mentioned my granddaughter in the introduction. She turned five this spring. That's a big birthday and, with her parents' permission, her Mimi and I decided to buy her a swing set for her birthday. We shopped and shopped, looking for one that would grow with her, yet one that would not break the bank. The one we ultimately bought has a couple of swings and steps leading to a small tower from which she can slide down the slide. Under the tower is a picnic table. As we bought it, we pictured her sitting at that table as a teenager, reading or doing her homework. Above that spot, we decided to write these words in permanent marker: "Dear Stella, this swing set is a small expression of our love for you. We hope you have many great adventures playing here. Love, Mimi and Papa."

When she saw the swing set for the first time she let out a squeal of delight. She ran to it and shouted, "Thank you Mimi and Papa!!! I love it!" Then she ran back to us and wrapped her arms around our necks and said, "I love you!" We pushed her on the swings, climbed into the fort with her, and slid down the slide. She was so excited about her swing set, she didn't want to go back inside for the rest of her birthday celebration.

As I stood pushing her on the swing, I thought to myself, *Could it be that just as we gave Stella this swing set as an expression of our love for her, and in the hope that she'd enjoy adventures on it, God created this amazing planet and gave it to us as an expression of his love? Was it intended for our enjoyment and adventures? How do we respond to a gift like that?*

Stella's response to our gift points to what is meant to be the most basic practice in the Christian spiritual life: We say to God, "Thank you!" and "I love you." It is the essence of worship and the most basic form of prayer.

Worship—and with it, prayer—is the first of the five spiritual practices essential to growing and maturing in our Christian walk. It was practiced throughout Scripture, lived by Jesus, and has been a foundation of the spiritual life for God's people across the millennia. God is worthy of and desires your worship. Your soul needs worship. You were created for worship.

Worship is the primary and appropriate response of the creature to the Creator.

What Is Worship?

Let's begin by defining what worship is. In her 1936 book, *Worship*, Catholic writer Evelyn Underhill offered this definition: "Worship, in all its grades and kinds, is the response of the creature to the Eternal." By the time I was in seminary this definition had been modified slightly: Worship is the primary and appropriate response of the creature to the Creator.

Underhill went on to say: "Nor need we limit this definition to the human sphere. . . . we may think of the whole of the Universe, seen and unseen, conscious and unconscious, as an act of worship." I love this. Everything that God created is a reflection of God's glory. When we look at the plants around us, they display God's glory. When we hear the birds singing or the bees buzzing or the lions roaring, they are, whether conscious of it or not, giving glory to God. When we see the maple leaves turning red and orange and yellow in the fall or the snow blanketing the earth in the winter or the dogwoods blooming in the spring, they all display God's glory. On a clear night when we look up at the moon and the stars, they, too, declare God's praise.

The birds can't help but sing. The stars can't help but shine. But we human beings, each of us unique in all creation, have a choice. We decide whether we will give thanks to God, praise God, and seek to glorify God with our lives, or not. But there is something within us that longs to worship, just as the birds need to sing.

I regularly try to thank my wife, LaVon, my employees, coworkers, family, and friends for the blessing they are to me. *"Thank you"* are two of the most important words you'll say in life. *"I love you"* are three more. If it is important to express that to those around you, how much more so to regularly express this to the Source of everything that exists, who designed all that is, who sustains it by his power and from whom, in an ultimate sense, all blessings flow? We were created as objects of God's love and affection, but, like the rest of the work of his hands, we're also created to give glory to God.

The earliest expressions of worship recorded in Scripture involved bringing an offering to God (see Genesis 4) or sacrificing something from one's crops or flocks as an expression of gratitude and love for God. This is not unlike the reasons we buy one another gifts. Some give gifts to curry another's favor. But at their best, the gifts we give to others express our love and gratitude. The same is true of our worship to God—it is an offering we bring, given not to persuade God to bless us, but as an expression of our love for and gratitude to God.

In the New Testament, there are three Greek words that are most often translated as the English word "worship": *proskyneo*, *sebomai*, and *latreuo*. These signify bowing down or humbling oneself before another, demonstrations of reverence and awe in the presence of one who is greater, or the rendering of service to another. The same is true of the Hebrew words in the Hebrew Bible/Old Testament translated as worship. We hear this in the poetry of Psalm 95, "Come, let us worship and bow down! Let us kneel before the Lord, our Maker!" (v. 6)

The modern English word "worship" comes from an Old English word, *woerthship* (or *worth-ship*). *Worthship* suggests something or someone is recognized as worthy of honor. Worship is how we respond to a Creator who is uniquely worthy of our admiration, our reverence, our awe, our thanksgiving and our praise. When we worship, we acknowledge God's glory, majesty, greatness, power, and goodness. We recognize and honor God as God, while recognizing that we are not God, but the children or creatures of God.

The Book of Revelation gives us a fascinating picture of worship. Revelation 4 describes the throne room of God, where God is surrounded by winged creatures as well as twenty-four "elders" representing the twelve tribes of Israel and the twelve apostles. All of them wear crowns. The winged creatures from time to time cry out, "Holy, holy, holy is the Lord God Almighty, who was and is and is coming" (Revelation 4:8). In response, the twenty-four elders, who have been wearing crowns, "Cast their crowns before the throne"—a sign of humbling themselves before God. They sing,

> "You are worthy, our Lord and God,
>> to receive glory and honor and power,
>>> because you created all things.
>>>> It is by your will that they existed and
>>>> were created."
>
> (Revelation 4:11)

Drawing upon Underhill's thoughts once more, worship is the appropriate response of the creature—humans, animals, inanimate objects, the universe itself—to the Creator who made them all, upon whom their very existence is contingent. We were made, in part, to give glory to God.

Back in the mid-1600s, Christian theologians in England and Scotland created a document called the Westminster Catechism to teach and summarize what Christians believe about God and what it means to be human. It was written in a question and answer format. Perhaps the best-known question posed in the Westminster Shorter Catechism was, "What is the chief end of man [or humankind]?" The answer: "to glorify God and to enjoy him forever."

We were created to display God's glory. Our lives are only properly oriented when we are seeking to give glory to God, honoring, revering, and recognizing God as the source of our lives. Our praise is not merely in words, but from the heart and with every part of our being. We are meant to be a *living hallelujah*. In seeking to give thanks, to praise God not only with our words but also with our lives, rendering our worship to God, we find communion with God and the grace, strength, and love to live as his people.

In what remains of this chapter, we'll consider two distinct dimensions of worship, both of which are important in the Christian spiritual life: worship together as the church and daily worship in the form of individual prayer.

Our praise is not merely in words, but from the heart and with every part of our being. We are meant to be a living hallelujah.

Worship in Community

We hear the call to communal worship as we turn once more to Psalm 95:6-7 (NRSV):

O come, let US worship and bow down,
*   let US kneel before the LORD, OUR Maker!*
For he is OUR God,
*   and WE are the people of his pasture,*
*   and the sheep of his hand.*

I've capitalized the pronouns to emphasize that this psalm is a call for the community to worship together. The familiar twenty-third Psalm, on the other hand, is an individual prayer: "The LORD is MY shepherd; I shall not want" (Psalm 23:1 NRSV). Both worshiping with others in community and individually in our daily lives is important. Walking with God involves both.

Let's consider our worship together as a community first.

While Jews and Christians might gather together on any day to worship, and many do gather daily for worship, there is one day of the week above all others on which Jews and Christians gather for worship. We call this day the Sabbath.

For Jews the Sabbath is Friday night to Saturday sunset, representing the seventh day of the week, set apart by God in the Ten Commandments as a day of rest and worship. This particular day is tied to the seventh day of creation, the day on which God himself was said to have rested. In Deuteronomy the Sabbath day is tied to the Israelite Exodus from Egypt.

Most Christians observe the Sabbath on Sunday, as this was the day when Christ was raised from the dead. Early Christians called it "the Lord's Day" as each Sunday was a time to proclaim and celebrate anew Christ's resurrection—the day on which Christ conquered evil, hate, sin, and death.

As we read the New Testament Book of Acts and the Epistles, we can piece together what Christians did when they gathered on the Lord's Day to worship. On that day they,

- prayed *with and for one another*, giving thanks to God,

- sang psalms and hymns and spiritual songs *together* to God,
- broke bread *together,* sharing the Lord's Supper as a way of communion with Christ and one another,
- confessed their sins to God and *one another,*
- reflected *together* upon the Scriptures and the stories of Jesus, that they might be more faithful followers of Jesus,
- sought to encourage *one another*, spurring one another to a life of love and good deeds,
- and collected an offering expressing love and gratitude to God while seeking to help others.

Thoughtfully planned worship will seek to incorporate all of these elements, and lead them in such a way that worshipers are able to understand and join in the worship.

Notice that these were all things that believers were offering to God and with one another. Worship was not something believers attended. It was not something they watched. It was something they *did*. They did not gather to be entertained, but to respond to God's love and grace with praise and gratitude, offering themselves to God and seeking to bless others. The pastors, musicians, and liturgists are not performers on a stage hoping to entertain the congregation. They are offering themselves to God to lead the people in authentic worship, seeking to bless God and to be used by God to draw the worshipers to God.

There is something about singing and praying, listening and connecting with others in worship that our souls need, and through which the Holy Spirit works. Jesus is present in this kind of worship in a way that we don't experience anywhere else. This is why, I believe, Jesus said, "Where two or three are gathered in my name, I'm there with them" (Matthew 18:20). Christ is with us always, but he comes to us in the music, in the preaching, in the praying, and in the other people around us when we gather with others for worship.

But I've also found that for me to best engage in genuine worship, what Jesus described as worship "in spirit and truth," I have to do more than just show up. I have to engage in worship. I find it helps if I arrive a bit early for worship. I pray on my way to church. I talk with others as I enter worship. I think about the words to the songs we sing. As the pastors pray, I spend time praying. I invite God to speak to me as the Scripture is read and the sermon is preached (on those weekends when I'm not preaching). I bring pen and paper to take notes and have my Bible with me to follow along. I ponder the meaning of the Eucharist and kneel as I receive it, praying and offering myself to God. My offering is an expression of my gratitude to God. And I leave remembering who I am and Whose I am, asking God to send me on his mission in the world. Before I walk out the door I reconnect with those around me. All of this *matters to my soul.*

There's one final thing to note about worshiping with others in community: this building of relationships and being in community with others remains important long after the worship service is over. We are meant to build relationships with others as a part of the worshiping community. Those relationships, built around our shared common faith, are critically important not only to our spiritual health, but even to our mental and physical health as well.

A host of studies have shown that people who are actively engaged in churches and other faith communities have better physical and mental health and live longer. There is something about being in relationship with others that we need, and churches and other faith communities provide not only significant relationships, but also support and care.

Worship connects us with God, and it connects us with others.

I'm writing the final revisions to this chapter from the surgery waiting room of Menorah Medical Center. My friend Chuck is sleeping on the couch. We've been a part of the same small group study at church for the last twenty-five years. He didn't get much rest last night as his wife, Mary, turned an odd way and broke her femur. She's in surgery as I sit here with Chuck, waiting for the doctor to come out to let us know how surgery went. Before I arrived, Peggy was here sitting with Chuck. Shortly after I arrived Kaye came to check in and see if there was any word. After I leave, Steve, another of our pastors, will stop by to check in. Meals are already being arranged for Chuck and Mary when she comes home in a few days. And all of these folks, with dozens of others, are praying, encouraging, and standing with Chuck and Mary as their church family. That's the power of being a part of a worshiping community. Chuck and Mary are ushers. They have friends they sit by. They have others they are in Bible study with. And that community matters. Worship connects us with God, and it connects us with others.

That leads me to an analogy for what we do in worship. My cell phone can hold a charge for about ten hours, though significantly less if I'm using a GPS application. If I forget to recharge it overnight, it's literally useless the next day. It turns into a very expensive paperweight.

Our souls, like our phones, need recharging. When we come together to worship, we are plugged into our Source of spiritual power. In the midst of giving thanks, praying and praising and opening our hearts to God, we experience the power of the Holy Spirit.

When we worship together, we lay our burdens before God, we ask for and receive his mercy, and we are filled anew with his Spirit. We hear his Word, our marching orders for life. We feast at the Table of the Lord's Supper. And then we leave renewed, inspired, and ready to serve God and serve others for another week.

Worship Frequency

Many Christians are worshiping less frequently than they once did. There was a time when committed Christians were in worship at least three out of four Sundays. Today it is, for many, closer to two out of four Sundays. Why is this? If you have children, it may be kids' activities or the stress of getting them ready for worship. I ran into a couple from my church yesterday who have triplets. They admitted that they worship with our congregation online more often than in person as it was just hard to get three infants ready for church.

For others who are empty nesters, it is travel on the weekends, to see the kids or to go to other places to enjoy their newfound freedom. For those who are older it may be health related. And then there is just the busyness of life. The fact that people can now find so many worship services broadcast on the internet makes it that much easier to miss gathering together as a community in worship.

I understand all of these reasons why we might miss being physically present in worship. We've had infants, then kids with lots of activities, and now empty-nesthood. But even when I'm on vacation, we've made being in worship a priority. There are times when we're out of town and cannot make it to church, and at those times I'm grateful that our services are live streamed online. But one thing online worship cannot give me is the community of people that are an important part of worship. For those who rely solely on online worship or television worship, you'll miss the community of people with whom you build relationships, who will teach your children in Sunday school or who will notice when you look discouraged or who will be there at the hospital when you are sick or who will sit with you after your spouse has passed. There's something important about being with people in worship that cannot be replaced by the internet or by listening to a sermon podcast.

So, how often should you be in corporate worship? Scripture points to every weekend. "Really," you might ask. "Every single weekend?" Yes, that is the goal I encourage you to set. One day in seven you begin your week gathered with God's people to sing, pray, listen, fellowship, feast, and offer your gifts to God.

It's not always possible to be in worship with the community every weekend—there are times I'm traveling, and I worship with a congregation in the city where I am or worship online. There have been a handful of times in my life when I was sick and could not make it to worship. But just as I take the time to eat two or three times a day, I make it my aim to join in corporate or communal worship once a week.

At Church of the Resurrection we use a little humor and childhood encouragement to help people make worship a priority in their lives. When we were in school, 90 percent or more on a test was an A, 80 percent a B, and so forth. In 2014, we began challenging our people to strive for an A in worship attendance—90 percent. This means missing five weeks or fewer each year. Worshiping with us online still counts. We then came up with a small sticker, something like the star we used to get on homework or tests when we were children in school. We put the small sticker, about half the size of a penny, on our members' name tags each year if they attend 90 percent of the time or more. The first year we had about three hundred people who had an A in worship attendance (we have attendance notepads people sign and we track this information). Last year the number was over one thousand who received an A in worship attendance!

This may seem silly or trite, but humans respond to positive reinforcement and accountability, and the sticker was a very small way to provide both.

Daily Prayer:
Our Individual Worship

So, one essential practice in the Christian walk is to participate in weekly worship with others. But corresponding to that corporate practice is the daily worship we participate in within our personal lives.

Our daily, personal worship is composed of both our prayers and our actions. In our prayers we praise, we confess, we petition God for help, and we give thanks. All of these are important, but for those who are just starting to pray, I tell them, the most essential dimension of prayer and worship is captured in just two words, "Thank you." In giving thanks we are recognizing that our life is a gift and this world is a gift and the air we breathe is a gift. Daily worship and expressions of thankfulness shape us to become people whose hearts are defined by gratitude.

By nature we tend to complain far more than we give thanks. A 2012 study involving two thousand adults found that only 52 percent of women and 44 percent of men take the time to express gratitude regularly (defined as at least once a week).[1] Maybe some people simply take their blessings for granted; it's easy to fall into that trap. Perhaps others regard expressing gratitude as a chore. If so, they miss something important.

Expressing thanks is important not only as an appropriate response to God but also for our own emotional, spiritual, and physical well-being. Giving thanks actually contributes to our health. Brother David Steindl-Rast, a Benedictine monk, put it this way: "It is not happiness that makes us grateful. It's gratefulness that

31

makes us happy."[2] This statement hints at the enormous power that gratitude offers for our lives. We're not called to give thanks because everything in our lives is going wonderfully. We're called to give thanks because our life itself is a wonderful gift from God. When we pause to recognize this and to give thanks, we find that our hearts are uplifted. Gratitude reorients us toward happiness, taking our eyes off of our complaints and focusing instead on the blessings we have received.

We're not called to give thanks because everything in our lives is going wonderfully. We're called to give thanks because our life itself is a wonderful gift from God.

Similarly, Dr. Murali Doraiswamy of the Duke University School of Medicine wrote: "If [gratitude] were a drug, it would be the world's best-selling product with a health maintenance indication for every major organ system."[3] Think about that for a moment. Dr. Doraiswamy is not a preacher or a theologian. He is offering a scientific assessment as a physician, professor, and clinical researcher. He is telling us that gratitude is healthful and that its beneficial effects are significant.

Other research bears out this claim. A study jointly conducted by the University of California San Diego and the University of Sterling in Scotland followed 186 patients with Stage B heart failure. One group in the study was asked to keep a gratitude journal over an eight-week period, writing down three things they were grateful for each day. The researchers concluded that those who kept a gratitude journal were less depressed, slept better, and had improved heart-related markers in the blood stream than the other patients who did nothing.[4] Dr. Paul Mills, the study's author, summarized the findings this way: "It seems that a more grateful heart is indeed a more healthy heart, and that gratitude journaling is an easy way to support cardiac health."[5] I love the idea of gratitude journaling. But even if you don't follow the discipline of writing it down, you can still have a pattern of daily prayer where you stop to give thanks. That's healthy too.

In a similar fashion, a study by Robert Emmons, one of the leaders in the field of positive psychology, at the University of California, Davis, and Mike McCullough from the University of Miami, looked at the effects of expressing gratitude over a ten-week period. The researchers found that subjects who wrote five things they were grateful for each week scored 25 percent higher in happiness than those who didn't practice this act of gratitude.[6]

For Christians, cultivating gratitude starts with giving thanks to God. My gratitude journals are always written as prayers of thanksgiving to God.

Several months ago, I had a conversation with a young man whose father was dying of cancer. The doctors gave his father only a short time to live. I asked the young man how he was dealing with the impending loss of his dad. He said, "Each night, I stop and list all the things I'm grateful for and give thanks to God for these, and it changes everything. I give thanks for what I have instead of what I don't have, and it gives me peace." That practice continued to sustain him after his father's death.

Paul would have endorsed that. He encouraged early Christians with these words: "Rejoice always, pray without ceasing, give thanks in all circumstances; for this is the will of God in Christ Jesus for you" (1 Thessalonians 5:16-18 NRSV).

The Christians in Philippi remembered how, when Paul first came to their city, he and Silas had been beaten and thrown in jail—and yet amid their suffering, as they sat beaten and bruised in a Philippian dungeon, they began singing hymns of praise. Years later, when the Philippians received a letter from Paul, in prison once again for his faith, they were not surprised that this letter would encourage them to "rejoice always" and not to worry about anything, but with prayer and thanksgiving to make their requests known to God. Doing this, he said, produces a "peace that surpasses all human understanding."

Prayer has a powerful impact on our lives, but we often neglect the practice. Forty-one percent of men and 59 percent of women in America report praying at least once a day. As part of the spiritual discipline of daily worship, I'd like to invite you to develop a habit of praying at least five times each day. These times of prayer might be as brief as pausing to say, "Thank you," but I'll also suggest a five-fold pattern of prayer below as an outline for further developing your times of prayer.

Regarding these five times of prayer, look to your fingers. Consider your thumb as your first time of prayer, when you awaken each morning. As I get out of bed, the first thing I do each morning is to slip to my knees next to my bed and pray. The next three fingers represent giving thanks at each mealtime. Your pinkie represents praying before you go to sleep at night.

My morning prayer begins with a word of praise to God, followed by thanksgiving for life, blessings and God's love. I ask for forgiveness, then pray for others. Finally, I offer myself to God inviting God to use me. I pray through my schedule for the day and ask God to make me a blessing to those I will meet with, or to use me in some way in each of the events on my schedule.

At mealtimes, I give thanks once more, and pray for my family and that God will guide and use me. Even if I am eating out, or eating with others, I give thanks. I may bow silently, or, if it seems appropriate, I'll ask those I'm eating with if I might offer a blessing (this is a bit easier to do when you are a pastor!).

Finally, at bedtime I'll pray once more, using a similar pattern to my morning prayers, offering praise, giving thanks, asking for forgiveness, praying for others, and offering myself to God.

Over the years prayer has become a regular and frequent rhythm of my life, something that happens spontaneously throughout the day. But making these five times of prayer a habit in your life will ensure that no matter how busy or distracted you become on any given day, you will have stopped to pray at least these five times.

Let me add here that Paul tells us to "pray without ceasing." Keith Green, a well-known Christian singer and songwriter who died in 1982, beckoned Christians to make their entire life a prayer to God. I found this image helpful. Many days I find that I'm in conversation with God dozens of times. But more than that, I'd like not only my words, but my very living to be an expression of praise, thanksgiving, and devotion to God. I want to be a living hallelujah.

Let your daily prayer life be an exercise in gratitude, humbling yourself and offering yourself to God.

Throughout this book I'll invite you to use your hands as visible reminders of these practices and setting goals for each. Let's start with how our hands might represent worship and prayer. Make a fist with your dominant hand. Allow this to be a reminder of pursuing the spiritual practices with others. Those five fingers represent worshiping and praying, studying, serving, giving, and sharing in community, with others. Now look to your non-dominant hand, unclenched. Allow your five fingers to represent five specific goals you'll have for pursuing this practice on your own.

As it relates to our first essential practice of worship and prayer, your clenched fist represents worshiping together in community. The fingers of the unclenched hand represent the five times each day you hope to pray on your own.

There are many patterns for prayer. At times I pray the Scriptures. I use the Lord's Prayer as an outline for prayer. But I've also found another way of using the fingers of my hand as a pattern for what might be included in prayer. Starting with the thumb, a basic pattern of prayer would include:

- **Praise**: I often draw from the Psalms in expressing my love for and praise to God.
- **Thanksgiving**: expressing thanks for the many blessings in my life.
- **Confession**: confessing my sins and asking God's forgiveness.
- **Petition**: asking for God's help and blessings for others and myself.
- **Yielding**: offering myself to God and inviting God to use me for his mission.

This five-fold pattern for prayer gives a broad outline for what might be included in your conversations with God. Using your fingers on your left hand as you pray helps you remember the five movements of prayer. Associate each finger with one of these acts. For example, petition is associated with my ring finger, a great tie-in as I pray daily for my wife and children. While I pray these five, I imagine placing my right hand in Christ's hand. The use of the hands and fingers are mnemonic devices. If they are helpful, great. If not, don't worry about them. But the five-fold pattern of prayer is something I've found helpful in my own life. There are others, but this seems somehow more complete than others that I've used.

That brings me back to Stella's birthday party. As the family gathered around—lots of aunts and uncles and cousins were there—we watched her open her presents. After each gift she opened, she would go find the person who gave her the gift and give them a hug. And then at the end of the evening, she wanted to say something to the group. She stood up in front of everyone and said, "Thank you, everyone, for my birthday."

That's a picture of what it means to worship. We accept and recognize God's love for us, God's gifts to us, and we say, "Thank you."

Now, to be honest, in the excitement of opening her gifts, Stella sometimes needed a reminder from her mother to thank the gift-givers. Her Mom (my daughter) would say, "Stella, what do you say?" To which she would reply, "Thank you!"

Sometimes we need reminders, too, which is why I wrote, and you are reading, this book. Sometimes we need someone to give us a helpful nudge and tell us: "What do you say for all the blessings that God has given you, for all the joy, for the sun that shines and the air you breathe?" And the most basic response is, "Thank you."

Worship together each week, and remember to give thanks five times a day, and you will be on the path to a closer walk with God, and making yourself a living hallelujah.

Lord, help me to see the beauty of this world you've given to us. Help me to notice the blessings all around me. Help me to remember that you are God, and I am not. Help me to trust that somehow you will see me through even the painful things in life and bring good from them. Grant me a grateful heart. Finally, help me to be a living hallelujah. In Jesus' name. Amen.

CHAPTER 2
STUDY

STUDY
THE IMPORTANCE OF LISTENING AND PAYING ATTENTION

Your word is a lamp to my feet
and a light to my path.
(Psalm 119:105 NRSV)

But as for you, continue in what you have learned and firmly believed, knowing from whom you learned it, and how from childhood you have known the sacred writings that are able to instruct you for salvation through faith in Christ Jesus. All scripture is inspired by God and is useful for teaching, for reproof, for correction, and for training in righteousness, so that everyone who belongs to God may be proficient, equipped for every good work.
(2 Timothy 3:14-17 NRSV)

41

Our little dog, Maybelle, is as sweet a dog as you could find. We live in a neighborhood out in the country. At night, before heading to bed, I let her outside to do her "business" one last time. Usually she comes right back when she's finished. But sometimes there are coyotes howling in the distance and her ears perk up. I can tell she's hearing the "call of the wild" and she wants to run to the pack of wild things howling in the dark.

I say to her, "Maybelle, c'mon, let's go inside. It's time for bed, sweet puppy. Come inside." She looks at me, she turns her head toward the coyotes, and she ponders. Again, I call her and this time I offer her a treat. "Maybelle, do you want a treat? C'mon, let's head inside." Usually the offer of a treat will get her heading to the front door. But sometimes, the call of the wild is just too great, and she runs off, barking as she runs full tilt toward the howls in the distance. And off I run after her hoping to save her from being eaten alive by the coyotes.

We've spoken of the Christian spiritual life as our walk with God. Among the most important disciplines of a follower of Christ is *listening for our Master's voice* and obeying his commands. Like Maybelle, we also hear other voices, aside from our Master, beckoning us. Those voices sound so alluring. But, like the coyotes crying in the dark, sometimes these voices are the sound of beasts that will devour us. They are a siren song that leaves us shipwrecked, or at the very least, lost and far from God.

In John 10, Jesus describes himself as the good shepherd and his followers as the sheep of his flock. Jesus said that a good shepherd, "calls his own sheep by name and leads them out. When he has brought out all his own, he goes ahead of them, and the sheep follow him because they know his voice" (John 10:3-4 NRSV). To be Christians involves following Jesus' lead and listening to his voice.

In this chapter we'll consider how we hear God's voice and how by doing so we are better able to follow and walk with our Good Shepherd.

General Revelation

How does God speak to us today? Theologians use the term "revelation" to describe God's self-disclosure or God's efforts to speak to us. Some theologians speak of two categories of revelation: general revelation and special revelation. General revelation (or natural revelation as it is sometimes called) is often used to describe what we learn of God from observing the world that God has made, including not only nature but the arts, our human story, and more. Special revelation involves God's direct action to speak to us—this includes the work of the Holy Spirit, the life, teaching, death, and resurrection of Jesus, and the Scriptures.

Let's consider natural or general revelation first.

Nature

The Psalmist looked up at night at the heavens, at a time where there was no light pollution, and he cried out,

> The heavens are telling the glory of God;
>   and the firmament proclaims his handiwork.
> Day to day pours forth speech,
>   and night to night declares knowledge.

There is no speech, nor are there words;
their voice is not heard;
yet their voice goes out through all the earth,
and their words to the end of the world.
(Psalm 19:1-4 NRSV)

I feel this same way when I gaze through my telescope at the night sky. The stars remind me how small I am and how great God is. They tell of God's glory. The apostle Paul notes, "Ever since the creation of the world his eternal power and divine nature, invisible though they are, have been understood and seen through the things he has made" (Romans 1:20 NRSV). Paul believed that even nonbelievers had access to the knowledge about God revealed in nature. The key is to be observant.

One year I planted a sizable garden at my house. Each day that I would work the garden, caring for the soil, fighting the relentless onslaught of weeds and insects, watering the plants in the midsummer heat, and finally bringing in the harvest, all spoke to me about the spiritual life, just as these same activities spoke to Jesus.

Jesus routinely saw in nature metaphors or illustrations of the kingdom of God. Mustard seeds, wheat, weeds, sheep, fish, fig trees, and yeast all figure into his parables. He had a keen eye for how the natural world reveals truths about God. I wonder, *In what ways has the natural world spoken to you, giving you insights into the spiritual life?*

The Arts

God has given human beings the ability to create art, music, and literature. What makes great art is the way it speaks to us, and particularly how it speaks to the human condition and the existential questions of our lives.

So often as I'm reading a great book, I feel it speaking to me about God. Often a scene in a film will be so powerful I find myself searching for pen and paper to capture the idea. I love to go to the theatre when I'm in New York. One year, after seeing two Broadway plays, I was inspired to plan a sermon series on "The Gospel on Broadway." Likewise, there are moments when a painting or sculpture speaks to me. I wonder if there is a book, a play, a scene in a movie, or piece of art that moved you and through which you heard God speak.

Through Life Experiences and People

As a pastor, I spend a lot of my time listening to people tell their stories. And in so many of their stories, I hear accounts of sin and redemption, fear and courage, despair and hope. I've witnessed people survive terrible tragedies, forgive seemingly unforgivable wrongs, and I've heard people rebound from terrible failures. God has used them to teach me.

So many of Jesus' parables involved seeing the Kingdom of God through the stories of people.

So many of Jesus' parables involved seeing the Kingdom of God through the stories of people: a shepherd searching for a lost sheep, a farmer scattering seed, an errant son welcomed home by a merciful father, and a good Samaritan immediately come to mind. But there were also the people Jesus observed and interacted with that became illustrations of the Kingdom: a rich young ruler, a prostitute who wept at his feet, a woman who gave her last two coins in the temple offering—Jesus saw each, and saw the truth about God illustrated through them.

God speaks through our everyday experiences and interactions with other people if we only listen.

Conscience, Intuition, and Reason

Finally, among those things we have described as general revelation, we find God speaks to us through our conscience, intuition, and reason. Our conscience is an inner sense of right and wrong. Closely aligned with conscience is intuition—a kind of knowing or sensing that is sometimes called a "gut feeling." These, coupled with our capacity to reason, are all means that God has given us to know God, to discern God's will, to sense right from wrong, and to perceive danger or opportunity. How does God use your intuition, conscience, and powers of reason to help you know his will?

Special Revelation

There are no doubt many other ways in which we can discern truth or know God's will that would fall under the heading of general revelation. Nature and natural revelation so often function sacramentally—that is, ordinary things become means by which we receive God's grace. But general revelation can also be misread or misunderstood—just observing the world around us does not guarantee that we'll draw the right conclusions about God's character. That is why special revelation, God's direct disclosure of the divine self and will, is important. We interpret and understand natural revelation in the light of this special revelation. Let's consider the ways in which God more directly reveals the divine self and will to us: the Holy Spirit, Scripture, and Jesus.

The Holy Spirit

Jesus promised his disciples, "The Holy Spirit, whom the Father will send in my name, will teach you everything and will remind you of everything I told you" (John 14:26). He also told them, "When the Spirit of Truth comes, he will guide you in all truth (John 16:13)." Throughout the New Testament we find God's Holy Spirit guiding Christians, something we believe still happens today.

But how does the Spirit speak to us? Most often, I experience the Spirit speaking in ways that feel very much like conscience, intuition, or reason as articulated above. The Holy Spirit typically speaks in a whisper, not a shout; through a nudge, not a shove. I've learned that I have to pay attention if I will hear the Spirit speak. I hear the whisper of the Spirit as I study, pray, read Scripture, or sit in worship listening to the choir sing or the band play, and as the pastor is preaching. And when I'm preaching, it is in my preparation for preaching that I hear the Spirit, and sometimes even as I'm preaching something will come to mind that seems important to share.

As when I'm preaching, at times a thought enters my mind that seems to come out of the blue. Perhaps it is to call someone or to go somewhere or to stop to speak to someone. At times it is a sense I have that someone is hurting or needs a word of encouragement. When I listen, pay attention, and actually make the call or go where I feel nudged to go or stop to speak to someone, more often than not I find myself in the midst of what some call a "God-moment" or a "God-incidence" (as opposed to a coincidence). This literally happens so frequently that I've learned to pay careful attention to the nudges.

But it is important to note that we're all a bit hard of hearing when it comes to listening to the Spirit. Our flash of insight may only be our subconscious. The word we hear from someone else may not be God's word to us but only their opinion. So we must test these insights, thoughts, and ideas to see if we're hearing well. This is what 1 John 4:1 speaks of: "Dear friends, don't believe every spirit. Test the spirits to see if they are from God because many false prophets have gone into the world."

How do we test to see if what we're hearing, sensing, or feeling is of the Holy Spirit? Having trusted Christian friends we can talk to is helpful in this. Talking to a pastor can be important. But ultimately, we turn to Scripture and the person, words, and work of Jesus to help us discern God's will and to make sense of the world around us.

Scripture

Among the most important ways that God speaks to us is through the Bible. Yet despite it being the best-selling book of all time, and Christians claiming all manner of authority for it, most Christians read the

48

Bible very little. A recent study found that 87 percent of all Americans own a Bible, but a majority of these had read little or none of it.[1] Another poll found that only 35 percent of Christians read their Bible weekly. But if we're serious about walking with God daily, knowing God and God's will for us, reading and studying Scripture will be a regular part of our lives.

Jesus not only read Scripture, he memorized it, prayed it, and lived it.

It is clear in reading the Gospels that Jesus not only read Scripture, he memorized it, prayed it, and lived it. As those who seek to follow him and walk with him, we should recognize that reading and studying Scripture will be an important part of our spiritual life. Let's consider what the Bible is, and then how we hear God speaking through it.

What Is the Bible?

The Bible is a wonderfully rich and diverse collection of writings, composed over a period of approximately 1,400 years, including sixty-six documents (as divided in the Protestant Bible) in two "testaments"—what Christians typically call the Old Testament and the New Testament.

If you've got a Bible, pick it up and let's walk through it briefly. Find the Gospel of Matthew (your Bible should have a table of contents in the front). With your finger at the Gospel of Matthew, notice that everything to the left of this is what Christians call the Old Testament, but Jews call the Tanakh or simply the Bible. It is also often referred to as the Hebrew Bible. Everything to the right of your finger, starting with Matthew, is the New Testament. Unless your Bible has extensive notes and maps at the end, you'll notice that the Old Testament makes up about 75 percent of the Bible.

The Old Testament is the story of Israel and Israel's relationship with God. It was written by people who were inspired by the same Spirit at work in us, reflecting upon their experiences of God, and their understanding of God, in the light of their times. It was written over a thousand-year period from the late Bronze Age, through the Iron Age, and to the Greek and Roman periods roughly from 1400 to 150 BC. It includes masterful short stories, case law, epic battles, court histories, poetry, songs, prayers, wise sayings, and social and religious criticism by the prophets demanding that justice characterize the people's lives and society.

The New Testament is the story of Jesus, God's Son, the long-awaited Jewish Messiah, the Savior and King. He came to show us who God is, and who God calls us to be. It contains in the Gospels the only first-century accounts we have of the life of Jesus. In the Epistles, most of which predate the Gospels, it contains the theological and pastoral reflections of the earliest Christians about the significance of Jesus and what it means to be his followers. And in the enigmatic Book of Revelation it contains a call to faithfulness to Christians in danger of giving up their faith or compromising with their culture. The book offers a fitting end to the Bible, for it foretells a day when evil is destroyed, paradise is restored, death has been defeated.

I've heard the Bible described by Christians as "a love letter from God" or "the owner's manual" or sometimes with the acronym, "**B**asic **I**nstructions **B**efore **L**eaving **E**arth." But even the cursory description of its contents in the previous paragraphs should make clear that it is not simply a love letter, it is not written like an owner's manual, and it is anything but "basic." It is a beautiful, powerful, complex library of documents that bear witness to the faith of its writers, their experiences of God, their insights and intuitions as they were led by the Holy Spirit.

If we are seeking to walk with and follow Jesus, then our view of Scripture should be shaped by his view. The Old Testament was Jesus' Bible; the New Testament was written after his death and resurrection and testifies to him. It is clear that Jesus read, studied, and memorized the Bible. He was able to quote it, and freely did. His life's mission was shaped by its words. His ethics, his theology, his spirituality were all shaped by Scripture. But we also see him challenging prevailing interpretations of Scripture, debating the meaning of Scripture, and at times even setting aside Scripture. We see him quoting some portions of Scripture frequently but have no record of him quoting or even alluding to others. He read all the Scriptures that make up the Old Testament in the light of two commandments: "You shall love the Lord your God with all your heart, and with all your soul, and with all your mind." He called this "the greatest and first commandment." The second commandment captured his ethic: "You shall love your neighbor as yourself." He went on to say, "On these two commandments hang all the law and the prophets" (Matthew 22:37-40 NRSV).

The apostles of the early church display a similarly complex way of reading Scripture. They were not biblical literalists. They, too, recognized the Bible's complexity. They were willing to debate it and reinterpret it in the light of Jesus and the two great commands. There were divisions in the early church over questions of interpretation just as there are today. But they read the Bible, memorized it, reflected upon their lives in the light of its words. Second Timothy 3:16-17 captures how the early church read Scripture, "All scripture is inspired by God and is useful for teaching, for reproof, for correction, and for training in righteousness, so that everyone who belongs to God may be proficient, equipped for every good work" (NRSV). Christians debate precisely what Paul meant by "inspired," but what is clear is that Scripture played a pivotal role for him, that it is meant to guide, teach, and correct us as we seek to walk with God.

How Often and How Much
of the Bible Should You Read?

I'd like to offer you several simple goals for reading Scripture. The first is to read it daily. Make this a holy habit in your life. After my morning prayers, the first thing I do is read the Bible. Second, start with a modest amount of Scripture to read. In chapter 1, I invited you to use five fingers of one hand to represent praying five times each day. Take a look at your hand again. As you get started reading the Bible, start with five verses a day, one for each finger. How long does it take to read five verses of the Bible? Not long. I'll give you some tips, below, for how to read the Bible and where to start.

Now, as you grow in Scripture reading and make this a habit in your life, I'd like to encourage you to up your game. Using the fingers on your left hand, how about five chapters a week? A chapter a day with two days to play catch up if you get behind!

Tips for Reading the Bible

I'd like to offer few tips to help you get started in reading Scripture if you're not already doing so regularly, or if you are, to help you get more out of it.

Start by finding a readable translation of the Bible, a translation in modern English. My favorites are the Common English Bible (CEB), the New Revised Standard Version (NRSV), and the New International Version (NIV). Next, look for one of these versions in a study Bible. A good study Bible has introductions to each book of the Bible that help you understand the historical context in which the book was written and its major themes, along with maps and other helps. At the bottom of each page, a good study Bible will have explanatory notes to help make sense of what you are reading. Among my favorite study bibles are the *CEB Study Bible*, the *New Interpreters Study Bible*, and both the *NIV Study Bible* and the *NIV Life Application Bible*. The first two study Bibles are from a more mainline theological perspective, while the latter two study Bibles tend to be written from a slightly more conservative theological perspective. All have excellent maps and notes in the back of the Bible.

Let's consider several common ways to read the Bible.

Reading for Understanding

We can read the Bible searching for information and understanding—we might read, for instance, the Gospels simply to learn about the life of Jesus and what he said and did, like we'd read a biography of some famous person (the Gospels are more than biographies, but we might read them in this way). Reading for understanding is important and as we do, it is helpful to have a good study Bible by our side to understand the historical context of what we're reading. One of the great things about many of the Bible apps available for phone or tablet or computer is that they have a host of study tools available to help in reading for understanding. One of the simplest classic tools is the use of cross-references— other Bible verses that speak to the same theme as the verse we're reading. One Bible verse often helps make sense of another.

"What does what I've just read tell me about God's will for my life?"

Reading for Formation

Another way to read the Bible aims to listen for God to speak through the text so that we are being formed by its words. When we do this we invite God to speak to us as we're reading a particular text of Scripture. We approach it hoping to see something of the heart and character of God, or to discern God's will as expressed in the biblical text. We might ask, "What does what I've just read tell me about God's will for my life?" A few simple questions I often ask when reading the Bible include:

- What does this passage tell me about God?
- What does it tell me about people?
- What does it tell me about myself and God's will for me?

Often, I'll make notes in the margins of my Bible as I'm asking these questions, or I might keep a notebook or journal, pondering the answers to these questions, and as I reflect and write, I often hear God speaking to me. If you are using a Bible app on your phone, computer, or tablet, many have a place to add notes at the end of each passage.

Praying the Scriptures

Many times, when I read the Scriptures, I find it helpful to turn the verses I've just read into a prayer. I'll take a short passage, read it, and spend time pondering its meaning using the first two forms of Scripture reading, and then I'll make the words of the Scripture the focus of my prayer.

Let's take a familiar text from Matthew 5:14-16, part of the introduction of Jesus' Sermon on the Mount. Listen to its words:

You are the light of the world. A city on top of a hill can't be hidden. Neither do people light a lamp and put it under a basket. Instead, they put it on top of a lampstand, and it shines on all who are in the house.

55

In the same way, let your light shine before people, so they can see the good things you do and praise your Father who is in heaven.

After reading and studying this text, my prayer might be something like, "Lord, help me to reflect your light for others to see. Help me to demonstrate kindness and compassion and love today. Use me to push back the darkness in this world. I pray that others might be drawn to you because of me."

I carry a pocket New Testament and Psalms with me everywhere I go. Among the best times for reading, for me, is when I'm taking long walks or exercising on the treadmill. As I read and walk, I will take the passage or verse I've just read and put it into my own words, making it my prayer. I did this with the book of Psalms recently, reading and praying one, two, or three Psalms each day while I walked. In this way I was literally walking with God.

Lectio Divina

Another very common way of reading Scripture in order to hear God speak through it is called *lectio divina*—Latin for "divine reading." The primary aim in *lectio divina* is communion with God through the reading of Scripture.

Lectio divina encompasses four simple acts or movements. It begins with a reading of the Scripture passage—*lectio* is the Latin word for "reading." I often pray before I read saying "Speak to me Lord, I'm listening." Less is more when it comes to *lectio divina*. Choose a short passage, a short story, or even a single verse. Read it and listen for a word or idea or phrase that seems to speak to you.

After the initial reading, I'll pray once more, "Speak to me, Lord, through this passage," then read the passage again, more slowly, this time aloud, thinking carefully about each phrase. In my Bible I'll underline words or phrases that seem pregnant with meaning. I'm listening more carefully this second time through. This step is referred to as *meditatio* or meditation on the text.

Next is a third reading of the text in a step called *contemplatio* or contemplation of the text. Here I read the text once again asking, "How does this idea, this word, this phrase, or text relate to me?"

The final step is called *oratio* from the Latin word for prayer. Here you enter into a conversation with God about the Scripture and the ideas you've been meditating upon and contemplating.

This pattern of Scripture reflection may be done in as little as ten or fifteen minutes, but if you have more time, you'll find the experience an even richer way to encounter God through Scripture. It can also be done with a group, where, after each step, the group discusses the insight or reflections gained at *lectio, meditatio, contemplatio,* and then the group may enter into a time of prayer with God.

Study with Others

As with each of the other spiritual practices we'll discuss in this book, reading and studying Scripture may be practiced individually and also with others. There is something very powerful about a group of friends coming together once a week, or every other week, to read Scripture, to reflect upon its meaning in the light of their life experiences, and sharing with one another their insights.

I have read the Bible daily and preached it for thirty-one years, but I still learn something new or hear God speaking in a fresh way through a Scripture as I sit with others studying the Bible together. Many of my closest friends are people I've spent years in Bible study with and from whom I've gained important insights into the Scripture.

It is instructive to remember that Jesus called twelve disciples to walk with him during his three years in public ministry. They became his closest companions and friends. He was, of course, mentoring them to carry on the work of the gospel. But he was also pointing us toward the importance of having friends with whom we study and listen for God to speak.

At the Church of the Resurrection we call these friends with whom we seek to grow in faith "stretcher bearers" based upon the story in Luke 5:17-26. A certain paralyzed man was brought to Jesus by his friends, who carried him on a stretcher. They hoped that Jesus would heal their friend. Upon arriving at the house where Jesus was teaching (Simon Peter's home!) they found the crowd around Jesus was so great they could not get in the door. So, they hoisted their friend onto the roof of Peter's house, ripped the roof off the home and lowered their friend to Jesus. These were true friends! And I love that Luke tells us that when Jesus saw *their* faith—not the paralytic's faith, but *his friends'* faith—Jesus decided to heal the man.

When Christians gather together in small groups, studying the Scriptures together, praying with one another, doing life together, they become one another's stretcher bearers and, together, they hear God speak to them.

My small group gathered last weekend to discuss the Bible. In the midst of this we began talking about a difficult situation one of our members was going through. Before we finished the evening, everyone in the group gathered around this member, laid their hands on him, and prayed for him. He said later that experience of feeling the support and care of his companions in Christ, his stretcher bearers, lifted his burden that day. God works through others to help us hear his voice, know his will, and to strengthen and encourage us.

I was speaking to a couple this week who lost their adult son several years ago. They said to me, "We don't know how we would have survived this terrible pain were it not for our small group. They were our stretcher bearers carrying us through this intense grief." This group of believers formed to study Scripture together, but as they did, they came to deeply care for one another and to live out the Scriptures by bearing one another's burdens.

When Jesus came to minister to the multitudes, among the first things he did was to invite a group of twelve people to join him as his small group. They ate together, studied together, prayed together, and grew together. If we are walking with Jesus, shouldn't we also have a small group with whom we're seeking to grow in faith?

Look once again at your hands. Clench your dominant hand. It represents pursuit of this practice of study with others. And the unclenched hand, consider this a reminder to read at least five verses of Scripture each day, stretching eventually to five chapters of Scripture each week.

Jesus: God's Word in the Flesh

I want to end by reiterating what I've suggested above, namely that the most definitive way in which God has revealed himself to the world is in Jesus. John writes in his epic prologue to his Gospel,

> *In the beginning was the Word*
> *and the Word was with God*
> *and the Word was God. . . .*
> *The Word became flesh*
> *and made his home among us.*
> *We have seen his glory,*
> *glory like that of a father's only son,*
> *full of grace and truth.*
> *(John 1:1, 14)*

When God sought to speak to the human race, to disclose who God is and who God calls us to be, he did not send a book, he sent a Person. Jesus was God's Word, God's message, wrapped in human flesh. Jesus once said to his disciple Philip, "Whoever has seen me has seen the Father" (John 14:9). All other words ever spoken or written about God are to be interpreted and understood in the light of this one word, "Jesus."

> *When God sought to speak to the human race, to disclose who God is and who God calls us to be, he did not send a book, he sent a Person. Jesus was God's Word, God's message, wrapped in human flesh.*

But how do we see and know Jesus? We know him through our life of prayer, our experience of him in our lives, and others' experience of him, to be sure. But our primary way of knowing Jesus—what he said, what he did, his heart and character and hopes for his followers—is through the New Testament, and most clearly and directly through the Gospels.

To that end, I've long taught our congregation that if you wish to follow Jesus, *you should read through at least one Gospel each year.* Every Lent I reread one of the Gospels, and often another throughout the year. I use the various ways of Scripture I've described above as a way of listening for God to speak to me through the words and witness of Jesus.

This entire book is about walking with Jesus, following him, yielding our hearts and lives to him, trusting in him, and seeking to do his work. But my relationship with Jesus is largely made possible by reading and meditating upon the Scriptures. They bear witness to this man I love. Jesus came to reveal God to us. And when I imagine God, I see Jesus.

Conclusion

After worship and prayer, if we would walk with God and become the people God wants us to be, we have to learn to pay attention and to listen. With the constant noise of life bombarding us, we often find it hard to hear the voice of God. But when we pay attention and listen in the ways I've described above, we find our lives enriched, and we hear God speaking to us in so many ways.

Scripture records what the biblical authors heard God saying to them as they listened to the Spirit. It is the testimony and reflections of God's people concerning their experiences of God's deliverance, God's discipline, God's grace, and God's will. It is the primary witness we have to God's Word that became flesh in Jesus Christ. As we read it, illumined by the Spirit, we hear God speak through it.

I end this chapter repeating this simple invitation: Open your Bible and read it, starting with the Gospels. Start with five verses a day, but, as you grow, consider five chapters a week. Read on your own. But also find or form a small group or Sunday school class to study and grow together. Do this and I can promise you will hear God speaking to you, you'll grow deeper in your faith, and you'll find yourself in a closer walk with God as you follow God's lead.

Prayer: Lord, teach me to listen. Help me to pay attention to the ways you are revealed in the world around me—in my everyday life. But also, dear Lord, help me to read and study the Scriptures, finding in them the words of life. In Jesus' name. Amen.

CHAPTER 3

SERVE

SERVE
HERE I AM, LORD, SEND ME

"Choose this day whom you will serve . . . but as for me and my household, we will serve the LORD."
(Joshua 24:15 NRSV)

"Whoever wishes to be great among you must be your servant . . . just as the Son of Man came not to be served but to serve, and to give his life a ransom for many."
(Matthew 20:26b, 28 NRSV)

"For we are what he has made us, created in Christ Jesus for good works, which God prepared beforehand to be our way of life."
(Ephesians 2:10 NRSV)

Several years ago three women at Church of the Resurrection, Rani, Leigh Marie, and Ginger, noticed that our furnishings ministry was receiving a large number of requests for children's beds.[1] As they looked into this, they learned that there were hundreds of children in Kansas City who didn't have a bed of their own. These kids were sleeping on couches or on the floor. Believing that a good night's sleep is important for children to do well in school, they felt God calling them to start a program focused on providing beds for kids from low-income families.

Enlisting the support of the church, and working with schools and social service agencies in low-income communities, they went about providing new frames, box springs, mattresses, pillows, sheets, and blankets to kids in need. Their vision: every child in Kansas City has their own bed. As of the writing of this book, there are 4,672 children who now have beds to sleep on because Rani, Leigh Marie, and Ginger saw a need and said to God, "Here we are, Lord, use us."

The Call to Serve

The third essential practice of the Christian life is serving. The words "serve," "serving," "service" and "servant" appear over one thousand times in the Bible. And most often in Scripture we learn that we are the servants of God. The Book of Joshua reaches its dramatic conclusion as Joshua, now aged and nearing death, says to leaders among the Israelites,

> *"Now fear [or revere] the Lord and serve him with all faithfulness. Throw away the gods your ancestors worshiped beyond the Euphrates River and in Egypt, and **serve the Lord**. But if **serving** the Lord seems undesirable to you, then choose for yourselves this day whom you will **serve**, whether the gods your*

*ancestors served beyond the Euphrates, or the gods of the Amorites, in whose land you are living. **But as for me and my household, we will serve the LORD.***"
(*Joshua 24:14-15 NIV, emphasis added*)

This is Joshua's primary charge to the Israelites before he died: Serve the Lord! But what does it mean to serve the Lord?

We learned in chapter 1 that *latreuo* is a Greek word that involves serving God through worship. This, as we have seen, is an important dimension of serving the Lord. But service is not only the act of worship, as important as that is. We are meant to serve God by doing his work and his will in this world. This is a simple but important truth: *God's primary mode of working in the world is through people.*

God's primary mode of working in the world is through people.

So we're meant to ask, What does God want or need us to do? We'll consider, in chapter 5, God's call for us to be his light, to share his love, to spread the good news of Jesus Christ. But in this chapter we'll consider the work we do to embody God's love and justice—the work we are called to do to heal the world and to help others.

In Genesis 6:6 we read that God looked upon the world he made, saw the evil and violence human beings were doing to one another, and "regretted making human beings on the earth, and he was heartbroken." That verse has always moved me—the injustice and evil in the world left God *heartbroken*.

When God looks at our world today, what are the things that continue to break his heart? When God sees pain and brokenness, poverty and injustice in our world, he is moved with compassion. And I think he cries out, as he did to Isaiah so long ago, "Whom should I send, and who will go for us?" And with Isaiah I believe each of us is meant to respond, "I'm here; send me" (Isaiah 6:8).

I've known Christians who seemed to believe that all that God wanted from them was to go to church, to pray, to read their Bibles, and to refrain from doing evil. But throughout Scripture we find that God calls us to do good, to practice justice, kindness, and love. When we fail to do these things, our worship and other acts of devotion are worthless to God.

Consider these words from the first chapter of Isaiah:

> *What should I think about all your sacrifices?*
>   *says the LORD.*
> *I'm fed up with entirely burned offerings of rams*
>   *and the fat of well-fed beasts.*
>   *I don't want the blood of bulls, lambs, and goats.*
> *When you come to appear before me,*
>   *who asked this from you,*
>   *this trampling of my temple's courts?*
> *Stop bringing worthless offerings.*
>   *Your incense repulses me.*
>
> *(Isaiah 1:11-13)*

The people were rendering their service to God—by bringing their gifts and offering their prayers and songs—but they were neglecting the matters of justice and mercy and kindness. So, God said:

Learn to do good.
Seek justice:
> *help the oppressed;*
> *defend the orphan;*
> *plead for the widow.*
>> *(Isaiah 1:17)*

Micah, ministering around the same time as Isaiah, offered his well-known response to the question of what the Israelites might do to please God:

"With what shall I come before the LORD,
> *and bow myself before God on high?*
Shall I come before him with burnt offerings,
> *with calves a year old?*
Will the LORD be pleased with thousands of rams,
> *with ten thousand of rivers of oil?*
Shall I give my firstborn for my transgression,
> *the fruit of my body for the sin of my soul?"*
He has told you, O mortal, what is good;
> **and what does the LORD require of you**
but to do justice, and to love kindness,
> **and to walk humbly with your God?**
>> *(Micah 6:6-8 NRSV, emphasis added)*

Similar words show up in other prophets, in the Psalms, and in the Book of Proverbs. Particularly meaningful for me are the words of King Lemuel in Proverbs 31:8-9:

Speak out on behalf of the voiceless,
> *and for the rights of all who are vulnerable.*
Speak out in order to judge with righteousness
> *and to defend the needy and the poor.*

Our older daughter, Danielle, is a public defender. She makes a fraction of what she could be making at a big law firm. She has about sixty cases she's carrying at any given time—more than anyone should have to carry. Ask her why she does it and she'll tell you she feels called to this work of ensuring that the poor have access to justice and that their rights aren't violated.

This is part of the lofty vision captured in the concluding line of the Pledge of Allegiance when we pledge allegiance to our nation, a nation that seeks to provide "liberty and justice for all."

It is impossible to be the kind of Christ-follower Jesus longs for without concern for justice and mercy for the vulnerable, the weak, the marginalized, the poor.

Jesus' first sermon was drawn from Isaiah 61 as he read these words, "The Spirit of the Lord is upon me, because the Lord has anointed me. He has sent me to preach good news to the poor" (Luke 4:18)

Jesus devoted much of his time to ministry with the poor, the marginalized, and the second class. He ministered with peasant people, with lepers, with the mentally and physically ill. He noted that, at the final judgment, people will be judged based upon whether they provided food for the hungry, drink for the thirsty, clothing for the naked and whether they visited the sick and the imprisoned and welcomed the foreigner (Matthew 25:31-46).

He noted that when we come alongside and help those who are in need, it is as if we were doing this for him. Likewise, when we fail to do this for those who need our aid, it is as though we had turned our backs on him.

Serving God Together

Among the many things I appreciate about John Wesley and the Methodist revival he launched in the eighteenth century was the way he held together the call to conversion and personal piety with a call for Methodists to be engaged in transforming society. True holiness was not simply about personally refraining from evil and doing good at the individual level. It was about loving one's neighbors, and that included not only the desire for them to be transformed by the power of Christ but also for them to have food and clothing and health care and education.

The early Methodists started schools and health clinics. Later, as Methodism spread to the United States, they started public schools, colleges and universities, hospitals and clinics, orphanages and day care programs. They launched ministries for the homeless, feeding programs for the hungry, job training for the unemployed, and thousands of ministries aimed at being the presence of Christ for their communities. Even the smallest United Methodist churches today seek to be engaged in efforts to heal our communities and help them look more like God's kingdom.

Methodists are not the only ones who did and continue to do this, but it is an essential part of the Methodist ethos and spiritual DNA.

I've known people who criticize "organized religion." But when I look at organized religion, I find it to be much more impactful than disorganized religion or solitary religion. I think about the hundreds of initiatives organized by members of the church I serve in which church members donate their time, talent, resources, even their blood, to help others. As I'm writing this, members of the congregation are serving on medical teams in developing countries; they are painting, repairing and building a playground for an urban school that doesn't have the resources to do these things. Members are providing free books through our Bookmobile. Others are working on our racial justice team. Some have drilled bore holes—wells—in rural African villages. Others are working in recovery and rebuilding efforts in flooded communities in Nebraska. These are just a few examples of ways in which we work together to serve God by serving others.

I'm also reminded that we each have a responsibility as citizens to speak up for the vulnerable and marginalized and to vote in ways that reflect our convictions. We're hesitant at times to speak up about politics, or to see the connection between our faith and our politics. Christians differ on *how*, not whether, we believe the government should be involved in addressing issues of injustice. A government will be concerned about its poor and vulnerable to the degree its voting people speak up on their behalf. In his powerful sermon, "A Knock at Midnight," Dr. Martin Luther King Jr. reflected upon the need for the church to speak up for the vulnerable and those experiencing systemic injustice and racism. He noted, "The church must be reminded that it is not the master or the servant of the state, but rather the conscience of the state."[2]

Walking with Christ, following him, means that we will be asking how we care for the marginalized, the vulnerable, the poor, and the powerless—those Jesus referred to as "the least of these."

Once more, the two great commands of Jesus form the basis for our understanding of what it means to serve God. "You must love the Lord your God with all your heart, with all your being, with all your mind, and with all your strength" (Mark 12:30) and "You will love your neighbor as yourself" (Mark 12:31). To these Jesus added a third, "You should treat people in the same way that you want people to treat you; this is the Law and the Prophets" (Matthew 7:12).

Notice this, that the central ethic of the Christian faith is love. Love of God. Love of neighbor. Love expressed by doing to others what we would want them to do to us. Paul, too, says the Law is summed up in the command to love our neighbor, then tells the Corinthian Christians that, without love, one is merely a "clanging gong or a clashing symbol (1 Corinthians 13:1)." The writer of Hebrews calls his readers to "provoke one another to love" (10:24 NRSV). James calls this the "royal law" of love. Peter calls his readers to "love one another deeply" (1 Peter 1:22 NRSV). John, in his first epistle writes, "Whoever does not love does not know God, for God is love" (1 John 4:8 NRSV).

This love is not a feeling, but a way of living and being. Practiced toward others, it is to seek the good of the other; to bless, encourage, care for, and serve the other. It is the essence of what Micah commanded, to do justice and to love kindness.

Doing justice, loving kindness, practicing love—these are intertwined. Doing justice entails practicing kindness. Practicing kindness is an expression of love and justice.

Here I Am, Lord

The Hebrew word Micah uses that we translate as "kindness" is *hesed* (or often *chesed*). It appears over 240 times in the Hebrew Bible and is an important word in Scripture. It is sometimes translated as kindness, sometimes as mercy, sometimes as steadfast or covenant love. It is often used to describe God's love for humanity. It is also used to describe an act of goodness the recipient has no right to expect—undeserved kindness—which is also one way to define the word "grace."

Grace is central to the Christian faith. We are saved, Paul tells us, not by our good works, but by God's grace, God's undeserved kindness. Jesus' life, death, and resurrection are the embodiment of God's grace. And if there is an attribute of Christ that we're meant to emulate it would be this kind of undeserved kindness and love shared with others.

I may struggle to see how I can have a significant impact on the injustice of the world, but every day, in multiple ways, I can make kindness my aim.

It's not difficult to practice kindness every day. But it does require intentionality, determination, and, well, practice. We talk about spiritual practices because we want to make them habits, but also because in order for them to become regular parts of our lives, we must practice them the way that great athletes or concert pianists practice their skills.

Each day we are meant to offer ourselves to God, inviting God to use us as his instruments of healing, justice, mercy, and love. I begin each day, after giving thanks, by praying some variation of the prayer Isaiah prayed upon hearing God's call, "Here I am, Lord, send me." Then my task is to pay attention to what's going on around me and listen for God's prompting and to respond.

How would your communities change if everyone in your church started each day on their knees, saying, "Here I am, Lord, do with me whatever you want"?

We see this orientation, this willingness to serve, in the story of Mary, a girl of perhaps thirteen or fourteen, to whom the angel Gabriel appears. He announces that God wishes to use her to give birth to the Christ. There were a thousand reasons she might have said no. And in a very real sense, the future of humanity hung on her response. But Mary said, "Here am I, the servant of the Lord; let it be with me according to your word" (Luke 1:38 NRSV). What would happen if that became our prayer every morning? How would our lives be different? How would your communities change if everyone in your church started each day on their knees, saying, "Here I am, Lord, do with me whatever you want"?

John Wesley compiled and edited a prayer that he invited the early Methodists to pray at the beginning of the new year, a covenant prayer, some variation of which I pray daily. I wonder if you might join me in praying this prayer right now?

I am no longer my own, but yours. Put me to what you will; rank me with whom you will. Put me to doing; put me to suffering. Let me be employed for you or laid aside for you, exalted for you or brought low for you. Let me be full; let me be empty. Let me have all things; let me have nothing. I freely and heartily yield all things to your pleasure and disposal. And now, O glorious and blessed God, Father, Son, and Holy Spirit, you are mine and I am yours. So be it. And the covenant I have made on earth, let it be ratified in heaven. Amen.

In this prayer we offer ourselves completely to God, and we invite God to use us for his purposes and glory. What does he desire to use us for? He's told us: to do justice and practice kindness or, in other words, to love our neighbor as we love ourselves.

In Matthew 20, two of Jesus' disciples came hoping Jesus would name them as his right- and left-hand guys when he claimed the throne in Jerusalem, something they were hoping he would do any day. When the other disciples heard this they were upset (I suspect because they themselves wanted to be on Jesus' right and left when he came to power). Jesus stopped and set them straight: "You know that the rulers of the Gentiles lord it over them, and their great ones are tyrants over them. It will not be so among you; but whoever wishes to be great among you must be your servant" (Matthew 20:25-26 NRSV).

In Jesus' day, when people wore sandals and walked on dirt roads, it was typical for them to take off their sandals and wash their feet before sitting down at the table to eat. If a homeowner had household servants, it would be the job of one of the servants to wash the feet of dinner guests. At the Last Supper, Jesus got up from the table, retrieved a basin of water and a towel, and washed his disciples' feet. Then Jesus asked, "Do you know what I've done for you? You call me 'Teacher' and 'Lord,' and you speak correctly, because I am. If I, your Lord and teacher, have washed your feet, you too must wash each other's feet. I have given you an example: Just as I have done, you also must do" (John 13:12-15).

To walk with God, to be a follower of Christ, is to be a servant, and one of the primary ways that we serve is to practice kindness toward others.

The Power of Kindness

As noted earlier, God's primary way of working in the world is through people. Paul tells us in Ephesians that we were created for this purpose, "For we are what he has made us, created in Christ Jesus for *good works*, which God prepared beforehand *to be our way of life*" (Ephesians 2:10 NRSV, emphasis added). Paul was not saying that we are saved by our works. We are saved by grace, through faith, not by our works. But good works—all of the essential Christian practices and especially works of service and kindness toward others—are our response to God's saving grace and means of growing in grace and living as God has called us to live. God created us to care for each other as members of the human family, to cooperate with him in sharing love, doing justice, and practicing kindness.

Interestingly, there is something about doing good works purely for others—and not for anything we might get in return—that actually blesses and heals us. In their book, *Why Good Things Happen to Good People*, Stephen Post and Jill Neimark describe an eight-week study involving 137 people who suffered from multiple sclerosis (MS). Some patients in the study met once a week with physicians who had experience in caring for people with this disease. Other patients received a weekly phone call from a fellow MS sufferer who simply offered support and encouragement. Post and Neimark note this study in their book because of a surprising result: the five MS sufferers who were phoning their fellow patients as part of the study showed improvement with *their* disease simply by offering encouragement to others. Giving support to others—kindness—had a therapeutic benefit for *the giver*. The research found a direct correlation between the helpers' well-being and the work they were doing to help others.

Mayo Clinic compiled some of the data from studies of the benefits of serving others by volunteering. The studies found that volunteering reduced the risk of depression. Volunteers were more physically and mentally fit. They had lower stress levels, something that contributes to longer life. These results are just what we would expect if God intended good works, kindness, and serving others to be our way of life. If we do what God actually meant for us to do, we have the "more abundant" life that Jesus spoke about.

Another study—this one by a group of sociologists—followed two thousand people for five years. The researchers were looking for factors in people's lives that correlated with happiness. So they focused on people who had reported that they were "very happy" over that five-year period. Those "very happy" people volunteered nearly six hours per month on average.[3] Yet another study, published by Carnegie Mellon University, found that adults over fifty who volunteer regularly had lower blood pressure than those who did not.[4] The scientific evidence is strong: serving others by practicing kindness is good for your health.

But serving others also shapes us spiritually. When we serve others, we become more like Christ. It's easier to be kind to others when we're already in a kind mood. But the truth is that service affects us most when we're not feeling that generous or gracious and we serve in spite of that. It rubs off on us and makes us more loving even when we're not feeling that way. It changes us.

Being Open to Divine Interruptions

There are great acts of service and tremendous sacrifices that others make that change the world. There are times when God calls us to this kind of service, the kind that might result in our giving up a great deal, perhaps even laying down our lives for another. But most often the call to service and kindness is lived out in many small ways on a daily basis. Sometimes it's as small as noticing someone who needs an encouraging word or the kindness of a smile and a hello.

Almost no one survives a jump from the Golden Gate Bridge. But Kevin Hines did. Kevin went to the bridge determined to take his own life. But when he actually arrived at the bridge, he was conflicted. As he began walking across the bridge, he told himself that he would not jump if even one person looked at him or smiled. No one smiled, reinforcing the idea that no one cared. Kevin jumped. He tells that the moment his body left the bridge he regretted jumping. He was one of the lucky few. He survived to tell about it.

Maybe he lived to tell about it so people might understand that just one simple act of kindness could have changed everything. The story reminds me that acts of kindness—the way we are meant to care for each other on a daily basis—don't necessarily involve work that is difficult or complicated. Sometimes, it can be as simple as paying attention to those around you, making eye contact, and offering a smile.

Part of what is necessary to serve Christ by serving others is our willingness to be interrupted.

Most often the opportunities to serve and show kindness are unplanned—they are interruptions. Part of what is necessary to serve Christ by serving others is our willingness to be interrupted. That sounds so easy to say, but it's hard to practice. We get so busy. We have so many things to do that haven't gotten done yet that we just don't have time for an unexpected interruption. We might not even notice the other person God has put in our path.

That's what is going on in Jesus' parable about the good Samaritan. You likely know it well. A man was beaten and robbed and left to die beside the road. As it happened, two deeply religious people came down that road, but instead of helping the injured man they crossed to the other side of the road and walked on by. Jesus doesn't say why they failed to stop. Maybe they were frightened, but just as likely, they felt they were too busy to help. Surely, they thought, someone else will stop to help.

Finally, Jesus said, a Samaritan came along. Though there was no love lost between Samaritans and Jews, the Samaritan was moved with compassion when he saw the man. He stopped to help. He poured oil on the injured man's wounds and bandaged them. He put the man on his own donkey and walked next to him to the town of Jericho, where he provided for his care.

Jesus told this story in Luke 10 to illustrate what it means to fulfill the second great commandment, to love your neighbor as you love yourself. It's clear from the story that love was not a feeling, it was a willingness to be interrupted, to take some risk, to give up one's own comfort, to be late for whatever engagement he had in Jericho, and to sacrifice something of himself to help someone else. This is what love and kindness look like.

John Lennon put into lyrics, "Life is what happens while you're busy making other plans." It's true. In Jesus' life, most of his ministry as recorded in the Gospels involved interruptions and Jesus' willingness to drop everything else. Jesus noticed the people who needed help. He didn't make excuses. He didn't pretend not to see them. He saw the interruptions as divine appointments, and they became some of the most important moments in his ministry.

Our congregation recently went through a strategic planning process, seeking to discern God's will for our church over the next decade. One of the four overarching goals was to help our congregation increase kindness and justice in our metro area. We aim to help every man, woman, and child in our congregation to pay attention, to offer their lives to God and for God's service each day, to see themselves as on a daily mission to do justice, and practice loving kindness in as many ways as they can, to as many people as they can. If you are a Methodist, this may sound familiar to you. It is the second of three "general rules" of the early Methodists who were to live their faith "By doing good; by being in every kind merciful after their power; as they have opportunity, doing good of every possible sort, and, as far as possible, to all men."[5]

A Daily Challenge

What if every person in your congregation were intentional about pursuing just one act of kindness meant to bless someone else each day, or even five acts of kindness each week? The average church in the United

States has about fifty people in worship. Let's do the math: 5 acts of intentional kindness every week, times fifty-two weeks is 260 acts of intentional kindness per person in your congregation each week. If you are an averaged size church of fifty people, that comes out to 13,000 acts of intentional kindness committed by your church every year. Is your church smaller or larger? Just multiply the number of people on an average weekend in worship times 260 to see what this challenge goal might mean to your community. This is God's strategy for changing and healing the world.

If we're serious about walking with Christ, we'll cultivate the daily practice of serving God by serving others. In your morning prayer each day, offer yourself to God's service. In chapter 1, I encouraged you to look at the five fingers on your hand and see them as a call to pray and give thanks to God five times a day, and, as a part of your prayer, to offer yourself to God's service. In chapter 2, I invited you to use these same fingers as a reminder to read at least five verses of Scripture each day (or five chapters a week). Now, take a look once more at your dominant hand with its clenched fist—allow this to represent the importance of serving with others through your church. And the unclenched hand with its five fingers: allow it to represent five acts of kindness pursued every week. Serve in and through your church and, five times a week, extend an intentional act of kindness toward someone else.

As you grow in the practice of paying attention and pursuing acts of kindness, imagine a time when this becomes five acts of kindness a day—five times a day when you blessed, encouraged, or helped someone else or when you spoke up for those who could not speak up for themselves.

How would your life be different if you were more intentional in your pursuit of the practice of serving God by serving others? How would your community be different if you and others in your church were together practicing thousands of acts of intentional kindness every year?

You can do this! In fact, you were created for this!

Prayer

Lord, you taught us that your glory is revealed when we, the human beings made in your image, extend your love and care for us to others. Make me aware of your "nudges." And give me a heart that is open to interruption when you need me. Amen.

CHAPTER 4
GIVE

GIVE
WHERE YOUR
TREASURE IS...

Do not store up for yourselves treasures on earth, where moth and rust consume and where thieves break in and steal; but store up for yourselves treasures in heaven, where neither moth nor rust consumes and where thieves do not break in and steal. For where your treasure is, there your heart will be also.

(Matthew 6:19-21 NRSV)

Give, and it will be given to you. A good measure, pressed down, shaken together, running over, will be put into your lap; for the measure you give will be the measure you get back.

(Luke 6:38 NRSV)

It is more blessed to give than to receive.

(Acts 20:35)

87

As we continue to explore the Christian walk and the essential spiritual practices that shape our hearts, we turn to the connection between money and the spiritual life. This may seem an odd topic—prayer, worship, Scripture reading, and even serving feel like spiritual activities to us. But money? Yet when we read Jesus' words in the Gospels we find that he speaks about money and material possessions more than he speaks of worship, prayer, and Scripture study *combined*. Jesus makes clear that our relationship with money can either sabotage our spiritual life or deepen and support it.

Your Tax Return Selfie

This last spring I was speaking to an accountant named Dan Hutchins. It was tax return time and he was in the midst of preparing his clients' taxes. As we spoke he said, "You can tell a lot about a person by their tax returns. A tax return is a kind of 'selfie.'" This intrigued me and I asked him to tell me more.

Dan, who is working on writing a book on the tax returns of America's presidents, said that most former presidents and candidates for president from the last fifty years have made their tax returns public. This is true of most vice presidents and vice-presidential candidates as well. He told me that most of these returns can be viewed online. With that he pulled up a tax return on his computer, the return of one of our nation's former vice presidents.

The return was from a few years before his run for office and it revealed an adjusted gross income of $200,000 for the family—a relatively modest income compared with most presidential or vice-presidential candidates. Then, digging a little further into the return, he found a very high mortgage interest deduction relative to the man's income. "This," Dan said, "tells me that this family was probably living on the very edge of what they could afford. So I'm going to guess that I will also find a very low level of charitable contributions, given that he was using an inordinate amount of his income for his house payment." Sure enough, the man gave $300 to charity that year—$300 from an income of $200,000 – about one tenth of 1 percent.

Dan went on to tell me how he and his associates had developed something called a "Tax Return Credit Score," a tool that lenders can use to analyze a person's ability to repay a loan. His research found that this calculation was actually a better indicator of a person's ability and likelihood of repaying a loan than someone's FICO score (their credit rating).

"We looked at defaults on home loans from 2008 to 2010, during the worst of the Great Recession," he explained. "People who defaulted usually had high enough FICO scores to get their loans, and enough adjusted gross income; those are the two things lenders tend to look at. But they were looking at the wrong information."

Dan went on to tell me that the tax return score they developed looks at the ratio of mortgage interest to income and looks at charitable giving. In fact, he noted, 90 percent of the tax return score is based upon charitable giving. He explained that the people who borrowed the maximum amount possible for their home loan were likely living at or beyond their means with little to spare. This usually meant that they either placed a low value on making charitable contributions, or they simply didn't have the money to do so. They also had no financial margin if there were unexpected expenses. Living at the edge of one's means, having no margin, and not placing a high value on giving were indicators that they might be at greater risk of defaulting. The greater the disparity between what they were paying in mortgage interest and what they gave to charity, the greater their risk of defaulting on their loan.

On the flip side, Dan said, "We found that people who were generous with their charitable giving were people who were, at least as far as we could tell from their tax returns, living below their means and showed evidence that they were thinking about others by their generosity. These people were significantly better credit risks than those who did not give."

What we do with our money tells us something about the condition of our heart.

I found all of this fascinating. It struck me that he was describing for me, in the language of economics and accounting, a lesson that Jesus taught in the Sermon on the Mount: that what we do with our money tells us something about the condition of our heart. Jesus said it this way: "Where your treasure is, there your heart will be also" (Matthew 6:21).

Hedonism:
Chasing after the Wind

Long before Dan taught me about the tax return selfie, my mother taught me that my bank account and my credit card statements are also a kind of selfie—a snapshot that reveals a lot about my life. Here Jesus' words from Luke 12:15 are essential to remember, "One's life does not consist in the abundance of possessions" (Luke 12:15b NRSV).

We live in a society where every voice around us is telling us just the opposite of Jesus' teaching—that our lives, in fact, *do* revolve around an abundance of stuff we own. Our culture tells us that, if we just had better, bigger, nicer, or cooler stuff, we'd be happier and more fulfilled. This morning as I opened my news feed there was an article about the ten watches every guy should own. I subscribe to *Car and Driver*, which regularly reminds me that my seven-year-old Mustang lacks the horsepower and new features of the latest pony car. When I check out Facebook, I find it has kindly displayed ads that offer me custom-made shoes and men's underwear, each promising they have the power to change my life. And, as a typical guy, I've got a thing for electronic gadgets, whether it's phones, tablet computers, cameras, headphones, or television sets, and each year there's a new model of each of these gadgets that makes the old model, well, old. The new gadgets whisper to me, "Your life really does consist in the abundance of your possessions."

Recently I had the privilege of spending time with Yale theologian Miroslav Volf as a part of the work he is doing on "a theology of joy and the good life." The "good life" is a phrase that's been around a long time. It's been used as the title of a British sitcom, films, novels, and popular songs recorded by artists ranging from crooner Tony Bennett to rapper Kanye West. The phrase is shorthand for a fulfilling, satisfying, and happy life. For many the good life is defined as having ample money, material possessions, and leisure time. And beneath this common, modern definition of the good life is an ancient philosophy the Greeks called hedonism.

Hedonism, drawn from the Greek word for pleasure, is a philosophy that taught that the highest good is pleasure and that the chief end of humanity is to maximize pleasure and to minimize pain. In and of itself, seeking pleasure over pain isn't a bad thing. But if pleasure is your primary definition of the good life, and your primary aim in life is to pursue it, you will find satisfaction elusive and a deep spiritual life impossible to attain. This is why Jesus said, "You cannot serve God and wealth" (Matthew 6:24). When we make money (and, in a broader sense, pleasure) our primary aim, it becomes our god, and God becomes merely a means to an end.

We also quickly find, when we make pleasure and the acquisition of more, new, and better our primary goal, whatever pleasure is derived from our possessions tends to be short-lived.

Among the problems with hedonism is something that psychologists call "hedonic adaptation." You may not have heard the term before, but we've all probably experienced it. It begins with desire. We set our hearts on something we feel will bring us pleasure, satisfaction, or fulfillment. It could be a move to a new house or apartment, a new or newer car, a new computer, smartphone, piece of jewelry, or pair of shoes. We think about the item, shop for the item, then eventually purchase it. But shortly after we buy it, the joy of owning it dissipates and we find ourselves wanting something else.

No one in the Bible expresses the idea of hedonic adaptation better than the writer of Ecclesiastes. In the book, the author is referred to as "the teacher"— traditionally the author was thought to be King Solomon in his old age. Read the book and you'll find a man who has devoted his entire life to acquiring pleasure and escaping pain. Listen to how he describes his hedonic yearnings:

> *I built houses and planted vineyards for myself...I also had great possessions of herds and flocks, more than any who had been before me in Jerusalem. I also gathered for myself silver and gold and the treasure of kings and of the provinces; I got singers, both men and women, and delights of the flesh, and many concubines...Whatever my eyes desired I did not keep from them; I kept my heart from no pleasure.*
> *(selected verses from Ecclesiastes 2:4b-10 NRSV)*

If hedonism is the path to the good life, we would expect that the teacher in Ecclesiastes would be very happy. But instead, over and over again in the book, he repeats the refrain that all is meaningless, pointless vanity—"a chasing after the wind."

It's not that possessions or experiences can't bring us some measure of pleasure—they can. But when pleasure and possessions are what we live for, like the writer of Ecclesiastes we find that we have been chasing the wind. We can buy many useful things for our lives on eBay or Amazon, but we can't ultimately buy the good life there. Amazon's "fulfillment center," (where goods purchased directly from Amazon are shipped out) can't provide us with lasting fulfillment. So, if lasting fulfillment, contentment, satisfaction, and joy aren't found at Amazon and eBay, where do we find them? Asked another way, What are the keys to the good life?

Gratitude: Giving Thanks for What You Have

There are three habits or practices that actually play a key part in helping us to experience "the good life." The first was articulated by Stoic philosophers in the Greco-Roman world, and it is the opposite of hedonism. These philosophers believed that the really good life was found, not in a life of acquisition of those things you don't yet have, but instead in learning to want what you already have.

How do we cultivate a desire for what we already have? The answer is surprisingly simple, and was part of the focus of our first chapter. Wanting what you already have comes from giving thanks for what you already possess.

I'll give a silly but very real example. In August of 2012, I replaced my 2006 V6 Ford Mustang convertible with a new Ford Mustang GT convertible. My midlife crisis car with its more powerful 420 horsepower V8 engine left me grinning ear to ear as I started it up, listened to the rumble of the motor, then squealed the tires just a little as I pulled away from the dealership.

But two years after I bought the car, Ford redesigned the Mustang, giving it an independent suspension, a cool upgrade to the interior, a nice remodel of the exterior and another 15 horsepower. Several years later they bumped the power by another 25 horses. With each redesign and upgrade, my Mustang didn't seem nearly as "cool" as it had when I bought it.

Ford, like most car manufacturers, will let you go online and build the car of your dreams, then order it from a dealer. So in the fall of 2014 I went online and built myself a new Mustang, just to see what it would cost. But I resisted the temptation to buy it. My "old" Mustang was barely two years old and still under warranty. I have gone through the same routine almost every year since then; I build them online, but never actually order them. Every time I've thought seriously about it, I go out and look at the Mustang I have. I open the door and sit behind the wheel. I start it up and listen to the sound of the engine. I repeatedly remind myself: "I'm so grateful for this car."

Those simple words—words that remind me to be grateful for what I have— have saved me at least $40,000! (The purchase price, taxes, title, and insurance.) And because of that, I've had more freedom to give to causes that mattered to me, and money to save to create financial margin that reduces stress.

I'm not suggesting that you should never buy a new car, or that I will never buy another new car. But

I've found the Stoics were right. As you give thanks for what you have, you find contentment and freedom; you possess your possessions rather than your possessions possessing you.

As you give thanks for what you have, you find contentment and freedom; you possess your possessions rather than your possessions possessing you.

By the way, purposefully and regularly invoking this feeling of gratitude also works to help produce long and happier marriages as well. LaVon and I have been married thirty-seven years. Every day, I thank God for her, she thanks God for me, and that helps us to want what we already have in each other, rather than pondering how much happier we would be if we were married to someone else!

Living Purposefully

The second key to experiencing the good life is to live purposefully. The writer of Ecclesiastes found that a life of pleasure was meaningless. So, to find the good life, it stands to reason that we might look for what is *meaning-full*. What adds meaning to our lives? What gives us fulfillment and a sense of purpose every day?

For Christians, a significant part of the answer is following Jesus. It was he who said, "I am the way, the truth, and the life." Following Jesus involves seeking to do his will. As we learned in the previous chapter, his will includes caring for others and trying to heal the brokenness in our world. Which points to the truth of the previous discussion: we find meaning not in acquiring things, but in loving God with all our heart, soul, mind, and strength, and loving our neighbor as ourselves.

Victor Frankl was an Austrian neurologist and psychiatrist. He and his family were arrested by the Nazis and sent to concentration camps because they were Jewish. He survived four different camps, including Auschwitz. All but one member of his family perished.

While he was in the camps—these hellish places filled with despair—he noticed that some of the prisoners woke up each morning with the attitude that they still had something to live for, typically a sense of meaning they found in serving their fellow prisoners.

Frankl began developing a theory that gave rise to an entire new field of psychotherapy. He called it logotherapy. Based on his observations of life in the camps, Frankl concluded that human beings who found a sense of meaning in their lives dealt better with their bleak situation. They coped more effectively with depression, anxiety, and suicidal thoughts. They were mentally healthier when they believed they were living for some purpose larger than themselves.

In his best-selling book, *Man's Search for Meaning*, Frankl described the revelation that came to him while in a Nazi concentration camp. The prisoners were starving, freezing, and forced to march to a work site very early in the morning, before it was light. As they plodded along, stumbling over each other in the dark, Frankl began thinking about his wife and how much he loved her. At that point, he didn't even know if she was still alive. But the mental picture of her stayed with him until all he could think about was his love for her. That love kept him going throughout the difficult march and sustained him in the months that followed. Here's how Frankl explained what happened that night:

> A thought transfixed me: for the first time in my life I saw the truth as it is set into song by so many poets, proclaimed as the final wisdom by so many thinkers. The truth— that love is the ultimate and the highest goal to which man can aspire. Then I grasped the meaning of the greatest secret that human poetry and human thought and belief have to impart: The salvation of man is through love and in love.[1]

In that moment, Frankl was speaking of the love he had for his wife, but throughout the rest of the book it is clear that his insight applies more broadly to the love we have and live toward others.

That's the love that Jesus described when he taught, "No one has greater love than to give up one's life for one's friends" (John 15:13). In the New Testament the Greek word for this kind of love is *agape*. It's different from the Greek words for romantic love or the love between family members, though it can be used of both. It means a kind of love that selflessly cares for another. That is the kind of love to which Jesus calls us, and it is in living this life of love that we find meaning, hope, and life

God Made Us for Generosity

The last of the keys to finding meaning, happiness, and fulfillment—one of the keys to walking with God—is generosity toward God and others. This is, itself, one expression of *agape*. We were made for generosity. It is meant to be both the shape of our heart and the way that we live.

We were made for generosity.
It is meant to be both
the shape of our heart
and the way that we live.

As with all of the other essential spiritual practices in this book, we give individually and corporately. Among the most important ways we give together is through the ministries of the church to which we belong. There we give, together, and have resources not only for the work of the church that takes place inside its walls but also the work that takes place through the church in the world. When we individually give our tithes and offerings as an expression of worship and gratitude to God, we also make it possible for the church to have a collective impact on the world around us that is vast compared to what we can achieve alone.

One small example I think of from the Church of the Resurrection is the collective impact our congregation's generosity makes possible through our Bookmobile.

Several years ago, we purchased and outfitted a micro bus and transformed it into a mobile bookstore from which kids from low-income families in Kansas City are able to take home books for themselves. For these kids, books are often an unaffordable luxury.

Because reading is so important in developing a child's imagination, language skills, and cognitive abilities, kids without books at home are at a real disadvantage compared to other children. Research shows that if children aren't reading at grade level by the end of third grade, the odds of success tilt heavily against them. The likelihood that they will graduate from high school decreases, while the odds greatly increase that they will live in poverty and spend time incarcerated. That's why books matter so much in a child's life.

The Bookmobile is a place where these children feel the thrill of picking out their own books. They take them home and read them again and again, share them with friends, and pass them on to siblings. Last year, through the generosity of our members, we gave away sixty-two thousand books in sixty locations throughout Kansas City. Our hope is to give away more books this year.

The Bookmobile relies on the generosity not only of those who offer financial support but also on those who give their time. We have volunteers who drive the Bookmobile to these various locations in our area. I want to share with you what one of them said about this work:

> Volunteering for the Bookmobile brings me joy because I understand how important this is for these kids to improve their literacy.

100

To me, doing something to help kids who need a boost is priceless. There is such joy for us volunteers in watching the excitement of these kids coming to the Bookmobile. I grew up with advantages. And I know a lot of these kids don't have the advantages other kids have. When I help with this, I feel like I'm doing what I was put on earth to do.

There's a special joy that comes from hands-on acts of generosity, from being able to see and talk to the people you help. But so much of our impact together also comes from numberless individual acts on behalf of people we'll never meet. In whatever way they take part, those who are generous with their time and their financial resources are putting love into action and in doing this they experience the truth of Jesus' words, "It is more blessed to give than to receive."

Generosity and Joy

Here's what we know: when we are generous, we find joy. And just as we were made to practice generosity together, in community, God also means for it to be a part of the daily rhythm of our lives. It was Winston Churchill who famously said, "We make a living by what we get, but we make a life by what we give."

I met Arthur Brooks a couple of years ago at the Aspen Ideas Festival. Arthur served for about a decade as president of the American Enterprise Institute, and in the summer of 2019, he joined the faculty of the John F. Kennedy School of Government at Harvard and Harvard Business School. Back in 2006 he wrote a book called

Who Really Cares, where he noted that the most generous people in America are those who are religious; their faith motivates them to give not just to their churches or synagogues, but to everything else as well. Brooks's study of generosity showed that 91 percent of people who claim to be religious give to charity, compared with 66 percent of nonreligious people. Please note that nonreligious people can be generous; two-thirds of them make charitable contributions. It's just that a larger percentage of religious people make contributions.

In 2008 Brooks wrote a book called *Gross National Happiness: Why Happiness Matters for America—and How We Can Get More of It.* I was especially struck by something he wrote in the book: "To the extent that happiness can be 'bought,' it is with charity: giving of effort, time, and money makes people much happier."

Jesus taught the same thing but said it this way: "Give, and it will be given to you. A good measure, pressed down, shaken together, running over, will be put into your lap; for the measure you give will be the measure you get back" (Luke 6:38 NRSV).

What did Jesus mean by that? He wasn't suggesting that, if you put money into the offering plate, you will get $2 or $3 back for every dollar you give (although that is what some TV preachers will try to tell you). Rather, Jesus meant that there is something about giving that blesses the giver. It brings you joy and gives you a sense of fulfillment and meaning.

A multitude of scientific studies have reached this same conclusion: giving actually blesses the giver. Through their ability to study how different centers in the brain respond to various stimuli, scientists can actually see how this dynamic occurs. They have observed from brain scans that, when people give, it lights up the brain's "reward center" that makes us feel happy. At the same time, giving diminishes the amount of activity in the amygdala, which is the part of the brain that produces feelings of worry and anxiety. Giving reduces stress and increases the sense of well-being, thereby increasing health and longevity.[2] It even lowers our blood pressure.

Jesus was right when he spoke of the blessings of giving. The blessings span the gamut from health to meaning to fulfillment to joy. Just think about which brings you more joy: to open a gift, or to watch someone open a gift that you picked out especially for them?

Because we were created in the image of a generous God, we were created for generosity to be the regular rhythm of our lives.

We were created in the image of God, and God is generous — a generosity seen most clearly on the cross, where the selflessness and love of God were poured out for all humankind. Because we were created in the image of a generous God, we were created for generosity to be the regular rhythm of our lives. When we are generous, we walk closely with God, our generosity touches the heart of God and we become what God made us to be.

But we have to practice these things (that's why we call them practices). We have to work at generosity every day so that it becomes second nature to us.

What's the rhythm of your life when it comes to generosity? Are you stingy with your tips? Do you try to get people down to the absolute rock bottom when negotiating a purchase, or do you find a fair price for both the seller and for you? Do you give generously when there is someone in need? Do you resent being asked for money, either by your church or by others? Or do you look forward to being asked and having the opportunity to give?

Here's a way to help you get into a generous rhythm as you walk with God. Take a look at your hands. As you may recall from earlier chapters, you can use the five fingers on one hand to remember the spiritual practices of praying five times a day, reading five verses from the Bible each day, and showing kindness five times a week. Now, to these simple practices add five acts of special generosity a month. Don't think of five acts as a quota or a ceiling. Think of them as practice so you can do even more as generosity becomes part of your daily rhythm. The generous act might be a tip you give to a server that is bigger than normal. It might be an anonymous gift to someone in need. It might be a donation to a cause that matters to you. Whatever it is, cultivate generosity. And as with our other practices, there is a corporate component to our giving; we give to the church and its ministries. Remember: Your giving is a selfie that provides a portrait of the true you. And when you cultivate generosity, in the process you will come to see yourself differently over time, because the habit of giving changes us.

I saw a video recently that touched me. Just before Christmas a few years ago, filmmaker Rob Bliss conducted an experiment with a group of elementary school-aged children. They were all about eight or nine years old, and they all came from lower income families. As part of the experiment, the children were asked about what they'd like for Christmas. One girl wanted a computer. "A big giant Barbie house," said another. One boy wanted a trophy case, and another wanted an Xbox 360, and yet another asked for Minecraft Legos. Then each of the children was asked what they thought their parents would want for Christmas.

"My mom would probably want a ring," said one of the boys. "She's never really had a ring." A new car, said another of the children. Watches and jewelry, others said.

Then, the camera caught the wide-eyed astonishment of one of the boys as he watched the organizers of the experiment present him with the Xbox he had mentioned. All of the other children had similar reactions when they received the gift they had been hoping for.

Then things took an unexpected twist. Each child also received the gift they had indicated their mother or dad would want. There was a catch. They could only keep one gift—either the one they wanted or the one for their parent.

The video showed what happened next. With little hesitation, each child chose to forgo a gift for themselves in favor of a gift for their parent.

The interviewer asked the boy who had asked for Legos why he made the choice to forgo the Legos and, instead, to accept the gift he thought his mother would want. He said, "Because Legos don't matter," the boy replied. "Your family matters. Not the Legos, not toys. Your family."

"I get gifts every year from my family," said one of the girls, who chose a coffeemaker for her mom over a new doll for herself. "And my Mom [doesn't] get anything." Another chose her mom's gift and said, "She helps me when I'm sick. She helps me with my homework."

"She gave me a house to live in," said one of the boys of his mother.

Said another: "[My parents] look out for me and do stuff for me, so I need to give back to them."[3]

These young children had already learned something that we may forget as adults: that it really is, as Jesus said, "More blessed to give than to receive." They inherently knew that we were made for generosity and that we find the greatest joy in life when we are selfless.

How Much Should I Give to God?

I became a Christian as a freshman in high school. At that time I was working part-time at a fast-food restaurant. My checks were about $75 per week. As I joined the church I asked my pastor how much I should put in the offering. He told me the offering was an expression of thanks to God, an act of worship and sacrifice that recognized that all of life was a gift from God, and that our offerings both honored God and made possible the ministry of the church. Then he taught me the concept of the tithe—giving the first 10 percent of what you've earned to God. I was a bit shocked. God wanted me to give $7.50 to him through the church *every week*?

We see the Old Testament law as giving us guidance, but we don't follow every part of the law. I was certain I could rationalize giving less. But I wanted to honor God and I decided to try giving the first 10 percent of my paycheck. Once I cashed my paycheck, the first thing I did was to put 10 percent in an envelope to give back to God on Sunday. To my surprise, I didn't miss the 10 percent, but I did feel joy in giving.

LaVon and I married right out of high school and, as we did, we committed to giving the first 10 percent of our income to God. I was attending college and working part time. She was working full-time. The first year we were married our income was $1,000 below the poverty level for a family of two that year. In addition, we had school debt. Yet we continued to give God the first 10 percent of our income. We always gave the first 10 percent, as we knew that if we waited to write our checks to the church last, we would never give 10 percent. Our tithes were an expression of our faith and of our intention that God be the first priority in our lives.

We never went without that first year of our marriage, nor at any point thereafter. At some point in college we began to give just a bit more than 10 percent away, supporting programs benefiting the poor. Over the years, as our income grew, we committed to give away an increasing percentage of our income. We give the first 10 percent to the church to support its ministries, but now give, above that, to a wide array of causes, much of which is focused on addressing poverty, helping with disaster relief and otherwise aimed at helping our world look like the Kingdom that Christ proclaimed.

Each year our tax return and our bank accounts are, for us, "selfies" that offer a snapshot of what is most important in our lives. Our giving is a form of self-denial, a form of worship, a means of serving, a way of recognizing that all of life is a gift, an attempt to give back, an expression of love and gratitude, and a means of following Jesus.

In Luke 19, Jesus enters the town of Jericho, just a few days before he will be arrested and crucified in Jerusalem. He makes his way to a sycamore tree in the middle of town, and he looks up to spot Zacchaeus, a chief tax collector (a wealthy man who had made his money by overcharging the people of Jericho for their taxes). Jesus looked up at him, called him by name and said, "Zacchaeus, I wish to eat supper at your house tonight." Zacchaeus was so in awe that Jesus knew his name, and wished to break bread in his house, that Zacchaeus could only think of one way to respond, "Look, Lord, I give half of my possessions to the poor. And if I have cheated anyone, I repay them four times as much" (Luke 19:8).

There is a clear connection between the relationship we have with our money and possessions and our spiritual life. Like each of these other spiritual disciplines, our giving both leads us to grow deeper in our faith, and it is an expression or evidence that we have grown deeper in our faith. Where our treasure is, there our heart will be also.

I've always appreciated the words of the apostle Paul, words he commanded Timothy to share with the wealthy believers in his church:

> *As for those who in the present age are rich, command them not to be haughty, or to set their hopes on the uncertainty of riches, but rather on God who richly provides us with everything for our enjoyment. They are to do good, to be rich in good works, generous, and ready to share, thus storing up for themselves the treasure of a good foundation for the future, so that they may take hold of the life that really is life.*
>
> *(1 Timothy 6:17-19 NRSV)*

In practicing generosity, we "take hold of the life that really is life."

Once again I invite you to look at your hands. The clenched dominant hand represents your giving to God through the church, where your generosity, combined with that of the others in your congregation, makes possible the ministry of the church and its witness in the world. This giving is an act of worship and Christian discipleship that reflects our love for and faithfulness to God. The fingers of the open hand represent five acts of extra-ordinary generosity towards others each month.

We're meant to practice generosity every day the way pianists practice a new piece until they know it by heart. When we practice generosity over and over, it becomes part of the rhythm of our lives, our hearts become attuned to God's desire for us, and we come to walk more closely with him.

Prayer

Thank you, God, for everything I have. I recognize that all of life is a gift from you. Please help me to become more generous, more willing to share with others. Help me to live beneath my means so that I might have enough margin to give. Help me to be generous toward you and others, remembering your unending generosity toward me. Amen.

CHAPTER 5

SHARE

SHARE
GOING FISHING, REFLECTING LIGHT

As Jesus walked alongside the Galilee Sea, he saw two brothers, Simon, who is called Peter, and Andrew, throwing fishing nets into the sea, because they were fishermen. "Come, follow me," he said, "and I'll show you how to fish for people." Right away, they left their nets and followed him.

(Matthew 4:18-20)

So we are ambassadors for Christ, since God is making his appeal through us.

(2 Corinthians 5:20 NRSV)

Go and make disciples of all nations, baptizing them in the name of the Father and of the Son and of the Holy Spirit, teaching them to obey everything that I've commanded you.

(Matthew 28:19-20)

Testifying

Have you ever recommended a favorite restaurant to a friend? I was boarding a plane for Kansas City recently when the flight attendant asked, "Any of you from Kansas City?" Many of us raised our hands. "I'm there for a couple of days and am told I should try the barbecue. Any recommendations?" Passengers became quite animated as they argued for Jack Stack, Joes Kansas City, Q39, Arthur Bryant's, Gates, or one of the hundred other barbecue joints in the Kansas City metro area. Kansas Citians love their barbecue and are certain we've got Tennessee, North Carolina, and Texas beat when it comes to the world's best 'cue. It struck me that my fellow passengers were all witnessing or testifying to something they loved.

An interesting thing happens when we talk about something that we love, enjoy, or find meaningful: the very act of sharing our positive feelings about the person, place, or thing actually increases our positive feelings even as we're seeking to share this good thing we're testifying about with someone else.

All of which is also true when it comes to our faith. As we talk about our faith, our experiences of God's love, of Christ's presence in our lives, of being a part of a church, of new insights into faith, or of the impact our faith has on our lives, we find our faith in Christ actually deepens and becomes more real to us. It is in giving away our faith, sharing it with others, that our faith and our spiritual passion grow.

When I talk to Sunday school teachers, Bible study leaders, or confirmation mentors in the church I serve, thanking them for their service, they nearly always respond in the same way: "I get far more out of doing this than those I'm teaching receive from me." I feel that way when I preach or teach—my faith becomes more real, my knowledge of and desire for God increase through the act of sharing my faith with others.

At a point in his ministry when John Wesley felt as if his faith was faltering, he asked the Moravian preacher Peter Bohler (sometimes spelled Boehler) if he should stop preaching until he had more faith. Bohler famously replied, "Preach faith till you have it; and then, because you have it, you will preach faith." He didn't mean that Wesley should be insincere; he was suggesting that the very act of talking about what little faith Wesley felt he had would serve to deepen his own faith.

This is why the fifth of our essential spiritual practices is sharing, testifying, or bearing witness to our faith. Doing so deepens our faith and love for God. But, of course, sharing our faith is not just about deepening our own faith; it is a missional imperative that comes from Jesus himself. When we share our faith, others come to see and follow Christ's light.

The Power of Reviews

We live in a time when sharing our thoughts, feelings, reflections, and recommendations about nearly everything is easier and more ubiquitous than at any point in human history. With the click of a button we can "like" something on social media or offer an emoji that captures our feelings about it. We are urged to write reviews on Yelp, Open Table, Google, or Amazon. Conversely, we also look to recommendations more than ever before. Before I buy anything or eat at any restaurant or watch any movies or television shows, I look to see how many "stars," positive ratings, or reviews are associated with whatever I'm considering buying, watching, or consuming. This is why today, more than ever, the most powerful and effective form of advertising is word-of-mouth.

It has never been easier to share our faith with more people, yet we're often hesitant to do it. Why is that?

Today, there are many people who are skeptical of faith, and even more skeptical of what is often referred to as "organized religion." Who can blame them? There have been more than a few bad reviews of Christians and churches. Read those reviews and you'll find words like "hypocritical," "judgmental," "irrelevant," "mean-spirited," "anti-intellectual," "anti-gay," and I'm sure you've heard many more.

These reviews don't reflect Jesus or the gospel he preached. They don't describe the church he intended. Neither do they reflect most Christians and churches that I know. But they do describe some Christians, some churches, and the unfortunate experience of some people.

Several years ago a friend sent me an e-mail announcing that she would no longer call herself a Christian. She had just had a conversation with a man who announced his faith to her, but then proceeded to share views that she found offensive and completely contrary to the gospel of Jesus as she understood it. She wrote, "I don't want to be associated with the faith this man was professing." So, she said, she would call herself a follower of Jesus but would not publicly identify herself as a Christian any more.

I told her I completely understood why she felt this way, and I agreed that this man's faith did not reflect the Christian faith as I understood it. But, I suggested, "If people like you stop calling themselves Christians, how will anyone know that there are any other kind of Christians than the kind reflected by the man you spoke with today?"

Most people who choose to follow Jesus do so because of the positive witness of Christians through whom they experienced love and from whom they heard a compelling witness and example of what it means to be a Christian.

None of us are perfect in how we live out our faith. But we are all called by Jesus to live and share our faith in such a way that others see him in us. The apostle Paul described himself and his colleagues as "Christ's ambassadors," and he believed that God was making his appeal to others through them. Jesus told his disciples to go into all the world and make disciples, teaching the things he had taught and baptizing others who would accept his call.

And just as people are sometimes turned away from the faith because of the witness of Christians, *most people who choose to follow Jesus do so because of the positive witness of Christians* through whom they experienced love and from whom they heard a compelling witness and example of what it means to be a Christian. In other words, most people who become Christians do so because of the "positive reviews" of others who have become Christians.

Jesus' Passion: Connecting with the Spiritual but Not Religious

We live in a time when an increasing number of people claim to be "spiritual but not religious." This is not new. In Jesus' time there were many who had spiritual yearnings but who had been turned off by the organized religion of his day. Jesus' passion seems to have been connecting with these people. When he called his first disciples, fishermen along the shoreline of the Sea of Galilee, he called them to follow him and to become fishers of people. That is still his call upon those who see themselves as Christians today—we accept his call to follow him and to fish for people.

In Matthew 9 we catch a glimpse of Jesus' heart for these spiritual but not religious people:

When Jesus saw the crowds, he had compassion for them because they were troubled and helpless, like sheep without a shepherd. Then he said to his disciples, "The size of the harvest is bigger than you can imagine, but there are few workers. Therefore, plead with the Lord of the harvest to send out workers for his harvest."

(Matthew 9:36-38)

I love this picture of Jesus: his compassion for those who were disconnected from God. He called his disciples to pray for God to send out workers into the harvest fields—a metaphor that, like fishing for people, had to do with drawing people to God.

Jesus was criticized for being a friend of "sinners and tax collectors." He befriended the broken, the sinful, the sick, and the demon possessed. This was his passion. Again, if we are walking with him we must see that he longs to draw people to God.

I love the story of Zacchaeus, the chief tax collector of Jericho (it appears he was short and had to climb a tree to catch a glimpse of Jesus). Jesus sought him out, invited himself over for dinner, and helped Zacchaeus find his way back to God. The story ends with Jesus explaining to the religious leaders why he was eating at the home of a notorious sinner: "The Son of Man came to seek out and to save the lost" (Luke 19:10 NRSV). This verse captured Jesus' life mission.

If this was Jesus' mission, is it not also to be our mission as his followers? And how can we claim to walk with him if we are not also pursuing his mission? As Jesus was preparing to leave this world he commissioned (co-missioned—inviting us to be in mission with him) his disciples, and through them, us, to continue the work he had begun, "Go therefore and make disciples of all nations, baptizing them in the name of the Father and of the Son and of the Holy Spirit, and teaching them to obey everything that I've commanded you" (Matthew 28:19-20 NRSV). In Acts 1:8 Jesus offers a similar call, "You will receive power when the Holy Spirit has come upon you, and you will be my witnesses in Jerusalem, in all Judea and Samaria, and to the end of the earth."

How Did You Come to Faith?

If you are a Christian it is because faith was shared with you by someone. For me the first person I recall sharing Christ with me was my grandmother, Sarah Hamilton. She was a devout Roman Catholic whose faith meant a great deal to her. She took me to Mass, taught me to pray, and gave our family a Bible that I eventually opened as a teenager and on whose pages I met Christ. She died when I was twelve, but I'll never forget her witness. I am a Christian today, in part, because of my grandmother's intentional efforts to share her faith with me.

I am also a Christian today because of a man named Harold Thorson, who went door-to-door inviting those in our new neighborhood to church. I actually decided to visit his church. There I met Phil Hollis, a young pastor who taught me about Christ, and Gary Patterson, a part-time youth pastor who mentored and encouraged me. I am a Christian today because of these men who took the time to share their faith with me. I have no idea who I would have been without them, but I can tell you that they had an incalculable impact on my life and the lives of everyone I've shared my faith with. How could I possibly thank them for the gift they gave to me? Each of these men has died, but one day I look forward to thanking them each for the life they gave to me.

Who is it that shared the faith with you? Take a moment and write their names down in the margin of this book. If they are still alive, consider writing them a note to let them know that they made a difference in your life.

Are there people who would say that you played a key part in their becoming a follower of Christ?

Here's the question I really want to ask you: Are there people who would say that you played a key part in their becoming a follower of Christ? Perhaps you invited them to church? Or shared your faith story with them? Maybe you listened and prayed with them? Or taught them in Sunday school, youth group, or Bible study? Or you were someone they knew was a Christian and you demonstrated an authenticity and love that led them to consider Christ?

If there is no one who would name you, it's not too late for you to begin to be more intentional about inviting or sharing your faith or bearing witness to what being a Christian means to you.

Today it is easier than ever for followers of Jesus to share their faith. Making a comment online is easy and nonthreatening, something like: "I was at church today and the sermon was about forgiveness. I really needed to hear this today." Or, "My kids really love their Sunday school class. If you don't have a church, know that you are welcome to join me!" Some of the best witnesses are photos of your serving with a team from your church, telling others about the work you and your congregation are doing to positively impact your community.

The power of the positive review is even more important when it comes to church than it is when it comes to restaurants or movies or books. With 280 characters on Twitter or a photo on Instagram or a few words on Facebook, you can talk about your faith in positive ways that help those who consider you their friend to know that you are a Christian, where you attend church, and how your faith makes a difference in your life.

Sharing Your Faith with Your Children and Grandchildren

We asked our staff at the church who was most responsible for their being a Christian today. Some mentioned friends, Sunday school or public school teachers, coaches, neighbors, youth pastors, and senior pastors. But the top answers were parents and grandparents. When I heard this I thought of my own granddaughter. LaVon and I pray for her multiple times every day. We are intentional about seeking to share Christ with her.

We pray with her at mealtime and bedtime when she is with us (we generally see her once a week). In addition to all the ways we play with her and mentor and teach her, we are also intentional about talking about our faith with her. I bought her a new children's Bible recently and we read and talk about these stories. I've been teaching her the Lord's Prayer, and as we learn it, I've realized that the prayer has some pretty big words that a five-year-old doesn't yet understand. So we've been talking about what "hallowed" and "kingdom," "trespasses" and "temptation," mean. It's been fun to not only teach her to memorize the Lord's Prayer, but what it means. Both LaVon and I took time to volunteer at Vacation Bible School recently so we could help her grow in her faith.

I think about my kids and how the most important gift I wanted to give them growing up was a deep trust in Christ and a desire to follow him. That would, I believed, shape the rest of their lives. It would give them a hope that would sustain them. A deep sense of purpose. A community of friends and stretcher bearers who would encourage them. I took them on mission trips with me, read them bedtime Bible stories, and tried to help them see Christ's love through my love for them.

I failed in many ways. I was at times married to my job and missed out on ball games or wasn't as fully present as I should have been with them. But, despite that, I hoped and prayed that they saw how much I loved them, even when my schedule and life were chaotic. And that even if they walked away from their faith at some point in young-adulthood, they would never forget their father kneeling at their bedside praying for them or seeing the ways my faith in Christ affected my life on a daily basis.

Both of our girls had periods of time as young adults when they were not interested in church and when faith took a back seat in their lives. I understood. When I was an adolescent, my family didn't go to church, so I found my own way by going to church. But my kids were in church all the time growing up. I could understand how, as young adults, they might step away for a time. But it was painful, and I felt I'd failed somehow as a parent to give them the one thing I most wanted them to have.

But during these times, I continued to pray daily for them, five times a day (as I still do). I would continue to talk about my faith with them. Sometimes I found it easier to write my thoughts down—my witness to them—in letters. I tried not to force my faith upon them during these seasons, but to show them lots of grace and a steadfast love regardless of whether they pursued their faith.

A woman named LuAnn was in my office recently. She began attending the Church of the Resurrection twenty-eight years ago. She had dropped out of church when she went off to college and was in her fifties when she finally began attending church again. When I asked her how she came back to church, she told me that it was a letter from her mother. Twenty-eight years ago, as her mother was battling cancer, she wrote a letter to LuAnn. She wrote, "LuAnn, you have everything a person could ever hope for—a caring husband, wonderful children and now a grandchild, financial success, a beautiful home. Yet the one thing that is most important in life, you are lacking. I long and pray for you to find a church and to walk with Christ." LuAnn told me, "When I received her letter it really made me angry. I was a grandmother by this time and my mother was still trying to tell me what to do." But LuAnn didn't throw the letter away. She kept it and, when her mother died several months later, she read it again.

It was about that time that Church of the Resurrection was starting and we were sending mailers out to the community. LuAnn received one of these and decided to visit this new congregation. Shortly after this, LuAnn, for the first time since she was a teenager, chose to become a follower of Jesus Christ. She's been following him ever since.

LuAnn reminded me of the power of a parent's witness, and how it may be years before a child comes back to faith. I wonder if you have shared with your children or grandchildren the importance of your faith? You might consider sitting down to write a letter, one that might be read again and again.

One last thought: I have written my daughters letters on their birthday since they were born. In each one I talk about my faith and my hopes and prayers for them. I saved these letters. When my older daughter became a mother, I bound these letters and gave them to her. I'll do the same for our younger daughter one day. My hope was that when I'm no longer here, they might go back and read these letters, remembering how much their father loved them and hearing once more a word about my faith in Christ.

What Is Your Church Known For?

As with each of the essential practices we've studied, faith sharing is not only something we do on our own, but something we do with others. Many people come to faith by first being invited to church. It is easier to invite people to church when your church has a positive reputation in your community.

How is your church thought of by the people in your community? What, if anything, is it known for? It is surprising to church people how little nonchurched people think about most of the churches in their community. If you drive past a building long enough, with no involvement with the congregation, it often becomes invisible—we no longer notice it as we drive by. That happens with many churches. The spiritual but not religious drive by and don't even notice the church. These churches don't have a bad reputation, they simply have *no* reputation among unchurched people.

Church of the Resurrection is hard to miss simply because of the size of both its building and its congregation. About ten years ago I asked our congregation, "When you tell people you go to the Church of the Resurrection, what do they say?" The number one answer was, "Oh, you go to that really big church." The challenge is that for three out of four people, being a very big church is not a positive. Three out of four people would say, "I could never see myself going to a church that big." In addition, there are often assumptions made about very large churches that are not positive.

I then asked our congregation, "What would you want them to say about your church?" I gave them a clue regarding my answer: "I'd like for people who don't go to church to say of us, 'That's the church with the big heart; the church that is constantly seeking to serve others, the church that is having a positive impact on our city and the church that welcomes everyone.'" Our people nodded. We were already trying to do this, but we began to redouble our efforts, not for the sake of our reputation, but to actually be the kind of church we believed God wanted us to be.

Nonreligious and nominally religious people are seldom interested in our worship styles, theological distinctives, or myriad of programs. These things matter, but they seldom are of primary interest to the spiritual but not religious. What leads the unchurched to take notice of a church is when that church and its members genuinely care about them and when they are actively engaged in seeking to have a positive impact on the community. They notice when a church serves others selflessly, when it gives generously, when it is loves radically.

This is what Jesus had in mind, I think, when he told his disciples, "Let your light shine before people, so they can see the good things you do and praise your Father who is in heaven" (Matthew 5:16). We are to let our light shine by our good works and those good works, Jesus said, were meant to lead people to glorify their Father in heaven—which is where we began this book, the idea that we are made to give glory to God. When others see our good works, when we've demonstrated radical selfless love, this can draw others to Christ.

In the last ten years the Church of the Resurrection has sought to live the gospel through acts of kindness, justice, mercy, and love. It is no longer just "the big church." In the last few years it has been recognized in Kansas City for its work in addressing racism. It was publicly recognized for its fifteen-year partnership with eight elementary schools serving in low-income communities where our members have invested tens of thousands of hours and millions of dollars. Local media has run stories about our house repair projects for the elderly, our ministry with special needs children and adults, our food drives, blood drives, and so much more.

Is Your Church Closing the Gap?

I once heard Professor Ron Heifetz of Harvard's John F. Kennedy School of Government talking about leadership. He drew a line with an arrow at the end, moving to the right. He explained that the line is the world as it is. Then, starting at the same beginning point as the first line, he drew a line up at a 45-degree angle with an arrow at the end, and he said the second line was the world

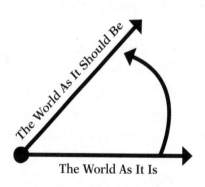

The World As It Should Be

The World As It Is

as it should be. Then he noted that leaders have the task of closing the gap between the world as it is and the world as it should be. This simple idea has been very helpful to me in thinking about church leadership.

Each church is meant to look at its community and ask, What would our community look like if, as we regularly pray, God's kingdom comes, and God's will is done on earth as it is in heaven? Using the Heifetz diagram, what should your community look like if it looked like the community Jesus hoped for (the arrow pointing up and to the right)? And where does your community fall short of that ideal? This gap between what is and what should be is where new visions are born.

Does your community need after-school programs for children? Or a food bank? Does it need a beds program or better support and partnerships with the schools? Are there immigrants who need a welcome? Elderly persons who need a visit? Are there people struggling with mental illness or loneliness or needing Meals on Wheels? I offer these few ideas only as a way of priming the pump for you to think about how you and your congregation could close the gap between the world as it is and the world as it should be.

Jesus told his disciples, "I give you a new commandment, that you love one another. Just as I have loved you, you also should love one another. By this everyone will know that you are my disciples, if you have love for one another" (John 13:34-35 NRSV). On the one hand Jesus is saying that Christians will be identified by their sacrificial love for one another, but I think Jesus intended more than that. Jesus repeatedly teaches us to love our neighbor and even our enemy. I think Jesus is saying that the church and her individual disciples demonstrate their faith with acts of love—not warm feelings for one another, but a selfless love that seeks the good of the other before good for oneself.

I was recently on a flight back to Kansas City from Atlanta. I was sitting in the middle seat. I struck up a conversation with the woman next to me, and in the course of our conversation she said she recognized me as the pastor of the Church of the Resurrection. She doesn't attend our church, but she described many of the things she knew that our church does to serve others in Kansas City. She ended saying, "I so appreciate all your congregation does to make Kansas City a better place."

As that conversation ended I went back to work on my computer, but the man on the other side of me spoke up. His next-door neighbors were two women, married and raising children. He'd been to our church for their children's baptisms. He loved these women and told me how grateful he was that our congregation welcomed them when others would not have. We had a great conversation about faith. After the plane landed and we were exiting the plane, the man looked at me intently and said, "I just want you to know your people really are the hands and feet of Jesus in Kansas City."

You might be tempted to say, Resurrection is a large church, but our church is smaller and we could not do this. But what I've described above can be scaled to any size congregation. If you are a church of fifty people in a community of five hundred people, your impact might be, relatively speaking, even greater than Resurrection's. Jesus created quite an impact with just twelve disciples who, with him, went about offering healing and hope and help for the people in the small towns and villages where they ministered. Your congregation, regardless of its size, can focus on closing the gaps in your community in a way that others take notice.

What do you hope your church would be known for in your community?

Invitational, Incarnational Living

Walking with Christ, then, includes being a part of a congregation that is seeking to be the body of Christ for its community and world, continuing the ministry that Jesus did when he walked on this earth: healing the broken, searching for the lost, announcing and embodying the good news of the Kingdom. *And* it includes daily seeking to be Christ's light and to share his light with others.

Yes, our most powerful sermons are those that we preach by our actions. But there also comes a time when we must use words. If you were to share the Christian gospel with someone else, what would you say?

As children we sing, "This little light of mine, I'm going to let it shine." This is part of our mission each day. We are meant to push back the darkness of suffering, inhumanity, pain, loneliness, injustice, and poverty. We do this both by our words and our deeds. You've no doubt head the quote, sometimes attributed to St. Francis of Assisi, "Preach the gospel at all times. When necessary, use words."[1] Yes, our most powerful sermons are those that we preach by our actions. But there also comes a time when we must use words.

If you were to share the Christian gospel with someone else, what would you say?

The great twentieth-century theologian Karl Barth wrote a series of books on systematic theology called *Church Dogmatics*—his attempt to explain the Christian gospel. The work spanned thirteen volumes and encompassed 2,500 pages. But when he was asked to put all of that theology into just one sentence, he famously responded with the words of a children's hymn: "Jesus loves me this I know, for the Bible tells me so."

First Peter notes, "Always be ready to make your defense to anyone who demands from you an accounting for the hope that is in you; yet do it with gentleness and reverence" (3:15-16 NRSV). How would you answer the questions, Why are you a Christian? What do you believe as a Christian? What difference does your faith make in your life?

Here's my attempt to answer those questions, given as a way of helping you think about your own story.

As a child my parent's sometimes took me to church, but it was my grandmother who told me about God's love. She not only told me, she lived that love. When I was eleven my parents divorced and when I was twelve my grandmother died. I decided I was an atheist. But at fourteen I was invited to church. I went, met cute girls there, and decided to return! But as I kept attending, I met people who shared with me their faith in Jesus Christ. I decided to try to learn more by reading the Bible my grandmother had given our family long before she died.

I'd never read or studied the Bible before, but I loved ancient Greek mythology, thought the Bible was ancient Hebrew mythology, and I decided to read it, cover to cover, my freshman year in high school. As I did, while hearing others talk about their experiences of God, I slowly began to believe there might be a God. I began to pray, and at times it felt as though there was really Someone who was listening. Eventually I began reading the Gospels.

I was taken with Jesus. His words in the Sermon on the Mount, the way he showed compassion for the sick, the hurting, the broken, and the forgiveness he extended from God to sinners—these things all intrigued me. I didn't understand everything I read at first, but the more I read, the more I came to love this man. I read Matthew, then Mark, and then Luke.

It was Luke's Gospel that won me over. Luke makes the point that Jesus was particularly concerned for the marginalized, the nobodies of his day, the picked on and pushed around. I loved that he loved sinners, tax collectors, prostitutes, Samaritans, lepers, and the like. That spoke to me. When I came to the end of the Gospel and read, now for a third time, that Jesus was crucified, died, and was buried, but on the third day he rose from the dead, I finally believed the story. I slipped to my knees next to my bed and prayed, "Jesus, I want to follow you. I know I'm just fourteen years old, but I give my life to you. Please use me and do with me whatever you want. I am yours." That was where my journey with Jesus began.

But it was only the beginning. Forty years later I still slip to my knees every morning and tell him once more that I want to follow him. I'm no longer fourteen, but now fifty-five, and I offer him, once more each day, my life. I love him now more than ever. He is the first person I speak to each morning and the last one I speak to before

I go to bed. His story has become my defining story. His words shape how I seek to live my life. His death expresses God's love and saving grace. His resurrection tells me that "the worst thing is never the last thing," and there is always hope because Christ has defeated evil, hate, sin, and death. I believe he walks with me always. The blessings in my life ultimately come from him. And one day, when I die, I hope to see him face to face.

I am a better husband, father, and boss than I would have been if I were not his follower. I'm far from perfect, but I think more of others and less of myself because of Christ. I give more of what I have because of him. I seek to love others in response to his call. I live with less fear and more hope as I trust in him. Following Jesus has changed who I am, how I treat others, how I spend my money, and my hopes and dreams—literally, everything in my life is shaped by my faith in Christ.

That's my elevator speech, my brief testimony as to why I am a Christian and what my faith means to me. But if I had to summarize it in a sentence, I'm not sure I could do better than Barth's summary, "Jesus loves me; this I know, for the Bible tells me so."

These preceding paragraphs are a summary of how I would share my faith story. Ask me tomorrow and I might offer this or that detail a bit differently, but the essential outline of this story would remain the same. I have shared it many times over the course of my life, and as noted in the beginning of the chapter, the act of sharing it makes me appreciate God's love and grace all the more.

The Challenge

I've invited you to use your hands and the five fingers on each as simple ways to remember the five essential practices and the goals for each. One last time, look at your hands. As it relates to sharing, your dominant hand represents the witness your church has together, the light you shine as a congregation within your community. The unclenched hand with its five fingers represents your personal practice and a goal of sharing your faith with five people this year. Those five fingers on your hand represent five people you know who don't attend church—many are the spiritual but not religious. Some are not even very spiritual. But each finger represents someone who knows you and with whom you may have some measure of influence—someone whose life would be positively impacted if they came to follow Christ. They might be your children and grandchildren, your parents or spouse, your next-door neighbor, or coworkers. Over the next twelve months, I'd like you to pray for them, to let your light shine before them by your good deeds, and finally, for you to either share your faith story with them, or at the very least, to invite them to church with you (Christmas Eve and Easter are great times to invite). Five fingers, five people, one year—that's the challenge.

The simplest way to start sharing your faith is on social media. Post pictures of ways that you are serving with others through the church. Share comments about your faith, insights you gained while in worship, or a simple invitation for people to join you in worship. As you do this, be aware of the kind of comments that might repel rather than draw non-religious people to Christ. A positive, caring, compassionate, and thoughtful comment about faith can be a significant witness for Christ. Conversely, political posts or posts that feel judgmental or hypocritical tend to turn people away.

Using social media moves way beyond simply inviting five people to church—you can bear witness to and invite your entire social network. Start sharing your faith via social media but include a goal of having five personal, face-to-face conversations about faith with others each year.

Go back and take another look at the names you wrote in the margin of this chapter, the people who helped you to know Christ or to deepen your faith. I'd encourage you to stop and thank God for them. And then to ask God to use you, that your name might appear on someone else's list years from now, as the person who shared your faith.

Prayer

Lord, thank you for your love for us. Thank you for the people you brought into my life who brought me to you. Thank you for giving them the courage to live their faith in such a way that I saw you through them. Bless them for the blessing they have been to me. Use me, Lord, as you used them. Let me be your light that pushes away darkness. Let me be your witness every day. Let me be a fisher who draws people to you. Let me be someone who allows others to see a reflection of you. Amen.

CHAPTER 6

THE FIVE PRACTICES FROM THE CROSS

THE FIVE PRACTICES FROM THE CROSS

"My God, my God, why have you forsaken me?"

"Into your hands I commit my spirit."

"Behold your son . . . Behold your mother."

"Father, forgive them, for they know not what they do."

"Today you will be with me in paradise."

"I thirst."

"It is finished."

My hope in this book has been to help us to close the gap between our spiritual lives as they are, and our spiritual lives as we hope they might be, or better, as God wants them to be. I want a closer, deeper walk with God. I suspect you also do or you would not have made it to chapter 6 in this book! We've considered five practices, some would call them spiritual disciplines or exercises that are foundational to the Christian spiritual life. They have been practiced by people throughout Scripture and across two thousand years of church history. These are:

- Worship (including daily prayer),
- Study (listening for God with an emphasis on Scripture reading),
- Serving (including acts of justice and kindness),
- Giving (generosity toward God and others),
- Sharing our faith (through deeds and words).

We've learned that each of these practices is meant to be pursued both in community with other Christians and individually in our daily lives.

At Church of the Resurrection these five practices form our membership expectations. We ask that every member commit to pursuing them before they join the church.[1] Within the Methodist movement, these five essential practices correspond, roughly, to the United Methodist expectations in our membership vows to participate in the church's ministries through one's "prayers, presence, gifts, service, and witness."[2]

I wrote this book anticipating that Christians and churches might read it during Lent and take up these practices as a way to prepare spiritually for the commemoration of Good Friday and the celebration of Easter. Lent has historically been a season for deepening faith and for taking on new spiritual practices. Fasting is associated with Lent and is one of hundreds of additional spiritual practices or disciplines that we did not address in this book. I think it fits under both worship/prayer and study/listening, at least as I practice fasting.

As I contemplated the conclusion of this book, particularly thinking of those reading it during Lent, I was drawn to the final words of Jesus as he suffered and died on the cross. I wondered if, in the seven last statements Jesus made, we might find evidence that Jesus himself pursued these spiritual practices. Before considering this question, let's begin with a word about crucifixion.[3]

Crucifixion

On that day we now call Good Friday, Jesus was tried before the Roman governor, Pontius Pilate, on charges of insurrection. He was beaten, taunted, condemned, and led away to die—death by crucifixion. He was forced to carry the *patibulum*—the portion of the cross to which his hands would soon be nailed—for as long as he was able, along the *Via Dolorosa,* the way of suffering. Upon reaching Calvary, a rock outcropping just outside the walls of Jerusalem, the cross was assembled. Jesus was stripped naked then his wrists were nailed to the cross, his feet were nailed, likely one into either side of the cross, and then it was hoisted into place.

We often picture Jesus' body elevated ten feet or more from the ground, but what little information we have about crucifixion would indicate that his feet were only two or three feet from the ground. Crowds gathered around to see the spectacle of execution. Jesus was crucified between two bandits. He was crucified at 9 a.m., and he hung there slowly dying until he breathed his last at around 3 p.m.

Crucifixion was a terribly brutal way to die—which is what the Romans intended. It was meant to deter other criminals or would-be rebels from committing crimes punishable in this way. By all accounts it was an effective deterrent. The more grotesque and cruel the punishment, the Romans reasoned, the greater the deterrent value of the act. Those who were crucified died a slow and painful death, sometimes taking a day or two to die.

Doctors have debated precisely how crucifixion kills its victims. It was likely the result of several factors including shock, loss of blood, and asphyxiation due to buildup of fluids around the heart and in the lungs. It was hard to breathe or talk while dying of crucifixion, particularly as death drew near. In order to breathe or speak, the victims needed to pull themselves up by the nails piercing their wrists, resulting in excruciating pain.

With such a struggle to breathe, it was even more difficult to talk. So, if one who was crucified spoke, it was at some cost. Especially in the latter stages of crucifixion we can surmise that most victims said little or nothing. Yet Jesus spoke seven different times.

The various Gospels record these seven utterances. Mark and Matthew mention only one of these statements, other than the reference to a loud shout as he breathed his last. Luke records three different utterances. John, three others still. Knowing the pain it took to speak, it seemed important to Jesus that he utter these words.

Knowing the Gospel writers preserved these utterances, the evangelists must have believed these words had some significance to Jesus' followers. As we turn to these statements, we'll see evidence that, even from the cross, Jesus was pursuing the five essential practices.

Worship ... Prayer

Matthew and Mark tell us that, near the end of his suffering, Jesus spoke, not to those around him but to God. Pulling himself up in order to catch his breath, he cried out with a loud voice, "My God, my God, why have you forsaken me?" This prayer, drawn from Psalm 22:1 (NRSV), is sometimes called the "cry of dereliction." It was one of three recorded prayers Jesus prayed from the cross.

The others, we'll discuss in a moment, were "Father, forgive them, for they don't know what they're doing" (Luke 23:34) and "Into your hands I commend my spirit" (Luke 23:46 NRSV).

It should not surprise us that three of the last seven statements Jesus makes before his death are prayers. He no doubt prayed as he began his day, as he approached his trial, and as he was being beaten and mocked by his tormenters, but these prayers are not recorded. The Gospels record that Jesus prayed frequently. Prayer was a part of the daily rhythm of Jesus' life. After he ministered to the multitudes, he "would withdraw to deserted places for prayer" (Luke 5:16). When he had important decisions to make, like the night before he chose his disciples, Luke tells us, Jesus "went out to the mountain to pray, and he prayed to God all night long" (Luke 6:12). We read of multiple occasions when Jesus gave thanks before he ate. He prayed on the mountains. He prayed in the boat. He prayed for the sick. He prayed for his enemies. On the night before his crucifixion he prayed, first for his disciples (John 17), then again in the garden of Gethsemane, "My Father, if it's possible, take this cup of suffering away from me. However—not what I want but what you want" (Matthew 26:39).

Jesus, too, had a moment in his life where evil seemed to have the upper hand and where God seemed conspicuous by his absence.

And then, after he was arrested, tried, beaten, sentenced to die, and crucified, he prayed from the cross. Let's consider this first prayer Jesus prayed, a direct quote from Psalm 22:1 (NRSV) where David first penned these words, "My God, my God, why have you forsaken me?" There is such pathos in this prayer. In that moment, Jesus found in Israel's prayer book the words that captured how he felt. He felt abandoned by God. David had felt the same way a thousand years earlier when he wrote these words. How grateful I am that the Gospel writers included this prayer, for there are times we all feel abandoned by God. And when we do, it is helpful and comforting to know that Jesus, too, had a moment in his life where evil seemed to have the upper hand and where God seemed conspicuous by his absence.

On the afternoon of Palm Sunday in 2014, I was home resting before returning to lead our Sunday evening worship. The phone rang and on the other end of the call, a member reporting the terrible news of a shooting at the Jewish Community Center. "Turn on the TV," said the caller, "I think these are members of our church who have been shot."

As the story unfolded, we learned that a white supremacist and former Klan leader from southern Missouri had driven to Kansas City, intent on murdering Jewish people. As it turned out, many of the people at the Jewish Community Center that day weren't Jewish; they had gathered there for a talent competition. Two of them, William L. Corporon, MD, and his grandson, Reat Underwood, were members of the Church of the Resurrection. They were shot and killed as they arrived for a rehearsal for the talent competition. From there, the white supremacist drove to Village Shalom, a Jewish retirement community a few blocks south of the Jewish Community Center, where he killed a nurse, Terri LaManno, who had just left from a visit to her mother. Terri was Catholic, and the aunt of one of our staff members.

As I sat at my kitchen table watching the news reports, I began to weep for these families, but my weeping soon turned to anger over the evil and hate of the man who killed them. I shouted at God, "Why didn't you stop him?" I've spent years helping people make sense of the problem of evil and suffering. I knew that God never intends for people to commit such barbaric acts. Genesis 6 tells us that God was heartbroken by the violence humans committed against one another. And I know that God doesn't typically intervene to stop evil people from doing evil things. God's own Son was brutally murdered by his detractors. God does not stop it, but at Easter, God overcame it. He ensured, by the Resurrection, that evil did not have the final word. I knew all of this, but on that day, as I sat watching the news, I found myself crying out with David and Jesus, "My God, my God why have you forsaken *them*?"

How did Jesus respond to the cruelty and inhumanity he himself was experiencing? He prayed. When being tortured to death he still prayed. As he felt abandoned by God he *still* prayed.

Throughout the Bible we find prayers like the one Jesus prayed from the cross, including a large number of the Psalms known as the "complaint psalms." The Book of Lamentations and the Book of Job also capture the cries and prayers of people facing tragedy. Jesus, David, Job, and the writer of Lamentations were overwhelmed with sorrow, yet notice, they still turned to God. And, as was the case with David and Job and the writer of Lamentations, the cry of abandonment Jesus articulated using Psalm 22:1 would not be the last of his prayers.

Study ... Scripture

The second essential spiritual practice we discussed was listening for God, particularly through the study of Scripture. Throughout the Gospels it's clear that Jesus saw the good news of the Kingdom in nature and in the stories and experiences of people. He had moments when he heard God speak directly to him. But it's also clear that everything Jesus said and did was shaped by his reading of his Bible, our Old Testament.

When he was tempted by the devil, he recited from Scripture. When he healed the sick, he fulfilled Scripture. When he preached, he cited, expounded upon and interpreted Scripture. His understanding of his mission was entirely shaped by Scripture. Hundreds of times in the Gospels by his words and actions, Jesus cites, points to, alludes to or fulfills the commands, hopes, and message of the Bible.

So it should not surprise us when two of the three prayers Jesus prays from the cross are from Scripture. Jesus prayed the Scriptures. As he hung dying on the cross Jesus prayed Psalm 31:5, "Into your hands I commit my spirit" (NIV). I love this simple prayer. It is a prayer that I often use in my own prayer time, an expression of complete trust in God.

Twentieth-century biblical scholar William Barclay noted that this verse of the psalm was a bedtime prayer Jewish mothers taught their children to pray at night, just as you may have been taught by your mother to pray something like, "Now I lay me down to sleep; I pray the Lord my soul to keep..." I love the picture he paints of Mary teaching little Jesus to pray, "Father, into your hands I commit my spirit" as he lay down to sleep. And there is something deeply moving to me when I imagine Jesus offering this prayer as he prepared to die, while his mother, who taught him this prayer, stood by.

"Into your hands I commit my spirit," is a prayer of absolute trust in God. The Greek word we translate as "commit" means "to entrust to someone for safekeeping." Jesus may not feel God's presence, but he entrusts his spirit to God anyway. In this he sets an example for us. When you're scared, when you're confused, when you're uncertain, when you're exhausted, when you're facing adversity, join Jesus in this prayer, "Into your hands I commit my spirit."

This is a simple prayer to memorize and to make part of your daily prayer life. When you need to let go of everything else and lay your life completely in God's hands, pray this prayer. When you are afraid and you're not sure what the future holds, pray this prayer. And as you pray this prayer you begin to feel what Paul describes as the peace that surpasses all understanding.

And as you study Scripture, you will find that you are, like Jesus, able to draw upon what you've studied in Scripture to guide, shape, direct and comfort you.

As you study Scripture, you will find that you are, like Jesus, able to draw upon what you've studied in Scripture to guide, shape, direct and comfort you.

Serving Others

The third of our essential practices is serving God, doing God's work and will while serving others. As with the others, this is meant to be part of the rhythm of our lives. We offer ourselves to God every day—asking God to use us, paying attention to see where others need our help, and then seeking to serve them through acts of justice, mercy, and kindness.

This is how Jesus understood his own life. He was constantly caring for, serving, and blessing others. He was the ultimate example of a servant leader. As we read in chapter 3, just a few days before he entered Jerusalem on Palm Sunday, he said to his disciples: "The Son of Man [which is how he often referred to himself] came not to be served but to serve, and to give his life as a ransom for many" (Matthew 20:28 NIV). The focus of his death was serving the world. He was the "suffering servant" the prophet Isaiah had spoken of, one who sought to draw all people to God by his act of redemptive suffering.

We see Jesus' servant's heart in several of his final utterances from the cross, but it is the words spoken to his "beloved disciple" John concerning his mother that I find so tender and moving. Jesus is enduring such terrible pain. His mother and his closest disciple stand near him. Seeing them there, he pulls himself up by the nails in his wrists and speaks first to Mary, then to John: "Woman, here is your son," and "Here is your mother." Jesus was dying, yet thinking about who would care for his mother.

I mentioned in chapter 3 that those who are married should notice, among the five fingers representing our acts of kindness, is the ring finger, a reminder that our kindness and service begins with our immediate family. Here, on the cross, Jesus reminds us that kindness and service include our parents.

Several years ago, as I read and pondered these words, I felt convicted, as if Jesus said to me, "I sought to care for my mother from the cross. Are you doing enough to care for your mother?"

I often get so busy I'm not paying attention to my parents' needs. It is sometimes easier to practice kindness and love for people who are strangers or parishioners than to think about my parents and their needs. Perhaps this is why the fifth commandment, "Honor your father and your mother," had to be made explicit, because we so often forget their needs. Jesus did not forget. The basic orientation of his life was that of giving his life away serving others. Our service to others, our kindness, starts with those closest to us.

I'm fortunate that my parents are both still alive. My dad lives in Seattle with my stepmom while my mom lives in Kansas City. I often get so busy, between pastoring the church; caring for my wife, children, and granddaughter; and speaking and writing, that my parents are at times lost in the chaos that is my life. My mother only half-jokingly says that the only way she gets to see me is to come to church. I wonder if Mary ever felt that way about her son?

As I ponder Jesus' words, I'm also reminded that John was not Mary's son. Jesus was asking John to take care of Mary *as if she were his mother*. When I meditate upon Jesus' words to John, I hear him calling all of us to care for those who are not our parents *as if they were* our parents. I think of elderly neighbors who need someone to come shovel their sidewalk when it snows, or someone just to check on them and say, "Hey, I was thinking about you today." Maybe it's an aunt or uncle who have no children of their own to check on them. Maybe they live hundreds of miles away, and it would brighten their day to receive a phone call from you.

Jesus' death on the cross reminds us that he saw himself as a servant giving himself to redeem the world. But his words from the cross about his mother remind us that his care was not only for the world, but for his mother. They call us to continue to care for our parents, and, like John, to care for those who are not our parents as though they were.

Are there people around you that Jesus is calling you to care for as if they were your own mother or father?

Generosity . . . Giving

We come to the fourth essential practice of generosity and giving.

We've learned that Jesus taught generosity throughout the Gospels. But on the cross, Jesus models what self-giving love and sacrifice look like. As Jesus noted, the Son of Man came to *"give* his life as a ransom for many." We see in Jesus' suffering on the cross the very definition of generosity and self-giving.

We're called to be generous and willing to share, to give ourselves away in service to God and others. We give a portion of our resources to support the ministries of our church. We also give of our time and talent. We're called to remember that from those to whom much is given, much is also expected. And, as God told Abraham, we are blessed to be a blessing.

Generosity and self-giving are at the heart of what's happening on the cross. John 3:16, sometimes described as the "gospel in miniature," is a verse that especially points to the generosity of the cross: "For God so loved the world, that he gave his only begotten Son, that whosoever believeth in him should not perish, but have everlasting life" (KJV).

We can see this self-giving in what appears, at first blush, to be a pretty mundane statement: "I thirst." If you've been with someone who was dying, you understand this. Often the dying have been unable to drink, so ice chips are placed on their tongues, or an oral swab, a small sponge on stick, is moistened and placed to their lips. So this statement from Jesus seems straightforward. Why does John feel compelled to tell us that Jesus said this? It is important to know that in John, mundane statements almost always are clues pointing to some deeper meaning.[4]

Earlier in the Gospel of John, Jesus and his disciples were passing near a town in Samaria. While the disciples went off to buy food, Jesus sat down at a well. There he met a Samaritan woman from the town who had come to draw water. Jesus knew this woman had been married and divorced five times, and now she was living with a man who was not her husband. She was likely one of the spiritual but not religious types who, because of her multiple marriages, had felt unwelcome in religious places. There in John 4, Jesus struck up a conversation with this woman, asking her for a drink of water.

The woman expressed surprise that Jesus, a Jew, would ask her, a Samaritan woman, for a drink. Then

Jesus said to her: "If you recognized God's gift and who is saying to you, 'Give me some water to drink,' you would be asking him and he would give you living water" (v. 10). What is this living water he is offering? It is life—a life lived with God, a life of meaning, and hope, mercy and love. Elsewhere Jesus uses the imagery of water to describe the Holy Spirit. It is all this and more.

The One who gives living *water is himself now thirsty.*
John means for us to understand that Jesus has poured himself out *for the world.*

John tells us this story early in his Gospel (chapter 4), and then he returns to the theme of thirst as Jesus hangs dying on the cross. Here's what I want you to see: The One who gives *living* water is himself now thirsty. John means for us to understand that Jesus has *poured himself out* for the world. I believe his thirst may be John's way of saying that Jesus has *given* everything he has. In quoting what is believed to be an early Christian hymn, Paul put it this way to the Philippians: Jesus "emptied himself."

The cross is the highest expression of generosity and self-giving. Jesus gave everything, the source of living water became thirsty, so that we might have life.

Witnessing to the Gospel

Finally, we come to the fifth essential practice, bearing witness to our faith so that others might find life in Christ. We are to embody the good news of God's love in Jesus Christ by our words and actions. This was Jesus' driving passion, his primary mission. This effort reaches its climax on the cross.

There Jesus proclaims the gospel, the love of God, with his arms outstretched saying, in essence, "This is how much God loves you. This is the lengths to which he will go to save you." Jesus said it this way in John 12:32, "When I am lifted up from the earth, I will draw everyone to me." His death was the most powerful witness he could make to draw people to God.

The Greek word for witness is *martus*: one who testifies to what they have seen. This is the source of the word martyr, which we define as one who dies for a cause or for their convictions because in dying for one's convictions, the person gives the ultimate witness. There is no greater form of witness than to die for what one believes to be true.

Jesus reached out to people who felt alienated from God and estranged from others. Shortly before his death he stated that his mission was "to seek and save the lost" (Luke 19:10).

He wanted sinners and broken people to know that God is the God of the second chance—rich in mercy, forgiving of even the worst things we could do. And so, he regularly associated with sinners and tax collectors and prostitutes, even though the religious leaders constantly criticized him for it. He came to tell them that God is like a shepherd who cares so much about each individual sheep that he will leave the ninety-nine who are safe to go rescue one that is lost. God is like the father who joyfully celebrates the return of his prodigal son who has squandered his inheritance and messed up his life; he wraps his arms around him and throws a party, saying, "My son who is dead is alive again." That's who Jesus showed us that God is.

Jesus saw his death on the cross as the climax of that ministry; by his death, God would demonstrate his love and forgiveness for all and forever. We're meant to look at the cross and to see a picture of the good news of God's love and redeeming grace. But in case we miss what the picture shows us, Jesus makes it plain with his words from the cross: "Father, forgive them, for they don't know what they're doing" (Luke 23:34).

Once more, Jesus is praying. But in this prayer, he's not praying for himself as he did in the two other prayers from the cross. Here he is interceding for others. Who was he praying for? He was praying for the Roman soldiers gambling for his clothing—the soldiers who had beaten, abused, and humiliated him before nailing him to the cross. He was praying for the Jewish leaders who, in their jealously and insecurity, accused Jesus of blasphemy and sentenced him to die. He prayed this prayer for those in the crowds who stood by on the street hurling insults as they passed by. He offered forgiveness to them all.

But even that is not all that's going on here. Jesus did not pray this prayer only for those who were taunting and torturing him. He prayed it for you and for me. And will God ignore the plea of his dying son? No, he will forgive, just as Jesus prayed. He will forgive your infidelity, your stupidity, your drinking too much, your lies, your pride, and your failure to love. He will, as you humble yourself before him, forgive the role you play in the injustice in the world, the harm you did, and the harm you could have prevented but didn't.

I love the insight that Tony Campolo offered when he spoke at Church of the Resurrection some years ago. He suggested that God transcends time and space; God is eternally present in what happened in the past, what is happening in the current moment, and what will happen in the future. And so, he suggested, as Jesus hung on that cross, he was peering into the future, seeing me and seeing you. He knew our names, he saw our faces, and he knew all of the worst things we would ever do. And, seeing us, he prayed to the Father to forgive them because they don't understand what it is they're doing.

As Jesus prayed for the forgiveness of others, one man nearby was deeply moved. He was a bandit—the kind of violent criminal who beat and left a man for dead beside the road in Jesus' parable about the good Samaritan. Jesus spent his final hours flanked by bandits who hung from crosses next to him. One of them began to hurl insults at Jesus. The other told his fellow bandit to be quiet—that unlike them, this man Jesus had done nothing wrong. Then he spoke to Jesus: "Remember me when you come into your kingdom" (Luke 23:42).

Elsewhere in the Bible, when God "remembers" someone, it means that God sees their plight and delivers them. I believe the man was saying, in essence, "Jesus, I don't fully understand the kind of messiah you are. But I just heard you pray for forgiveness for all those people. When you come into your kingdom, please remember me. Yours is the kind of kingdom I want to be part of."

Jesus indeed remembered him and spoke once more from the cross. He assured him, "Today you will be with me in paradise" (Luke 23:43).

To the end of his life, Jesus was still trying to rescue lost sheep, still demonstrating God's relentless love.

I love this scene. To the end of his life, Jesus was still trying to rescue lost sheep, still demonstrating God's relentless love.

As I read this story of Jesus and the thief on the cross, I'm reminded of Charles Wesley, the hymn-writing brother of John Wesley and cofounder of the Methodist movement. In his journals he records caring for those about to be hanged from the gallows. He would walk with them to the place of their death, singing hymns to them as they prepared to die. He wanted them to hear, as they faced death, that God was the God of the second chance, and that God loved them, and that to them, too, Jesus said, "Today you will be with me in paradise."

To the end, Jesus was trying to draw others, even those condemned to die, to Christ. I love this about him. This was his mission, his driving passion. Nearly everything he did was to this end. If we would walk with Jesus, we must find or cultivate within us this same desire to draw others to Christ, both by our deeds and by our words.

157

A Divine Drama, Enacted for Us

Now we come to Jesus' final words: "It is finished" (John 19:30 NRSV). In Greek, these three words are just one word—*tetelestai*—a word that means completed, fulfilled or accomplished. It is a word that describes the goal toward which everything is progressing. Bishop Will Willimon describes *tetelestai* as the kind of word we might have expected Michelangelo to exclaim when he placed the last brush stroke on the ceiling of the Sistine Chapel: *At last, it is finished! It is accomplished!*[5]

In English, "It is finished" may sound like a cry of defeat. But when Jesus musters the strength to shout, "*Tetelestai!*" it is not defeat he is signaling, but victory. He has accomplished what he came to do. He has given us a masterpiece, a divine drama in which God, through the suffering and death of Jesus, unmasks human depravity and reveals the depth of God's redeeming love. Isaac Watts captured the scene well when he penned these words:

> When I survey the wondrous cross
> on which the Prince of Glory died;
> my richest gain I count but loss,
> and pour contempt on all my pride...
>
> See, from his head, his hands, his feet,
> sorrow and love flow mingled down.
> Did e'er such love and sorrow meet,
> or thorns compose so rich a crown?
>
> Were the whole realm of nature mine,
> that were an offering far too small;

love so amazing, so divine,
demands my soul, my life, my all.[6]

And it is precisely because of that divine love that we long to walk with Jesus and invite Jesus to walk with us.

When we survey the wondrous cross, we find that worship and prayer, study, serving, giving, and sharing were expressed in Jesus' final words from the cross. There he prayed, recited Scripture, demonstrated service to others, gave himself for us, and sought to draw all people to God.

The cross of Christ displays a "love so amazing, so divine," that it demands our soul, our life, our all. It calls us to love God with all that we are and to love our neighbor as we love ourselves. The five essential practices we've studied in this book are each means of growing in our love of God and others as we seek to walk with Jesus in our daily life.

Prayer

Thank you, God, for loving me more than I will ever comprehend. Thank you for sending Jesus to rescue me when I have been lost. I accept your love, your forgiveness, and your grace. Help me as I seek to walk with you, my crucified king. In your holy name. Amen.

POSTSCRIPT
A FINAL CHALLENGE

Most of us know we should exercise, but the Center for Disease Control says that only 23 percent of Americans exercise as they should. I noted in the introduction that I spent years getting *out of* shape by eating poorly and seldom exercising. I knew I *should* exercise and eat better, but knowing and doing are two different things. It finally caught up with me, a fact I realized when I couldn't keep up with my wife and daughter on a moderately strenuous walk.

It's funny, the exercises that got me back in shape weren't difficult or complicated. I began with seven minutes a day of exercises I learned in elementary school, eventually adding brisk walks, and finally upping the quantity of exercise to the amount the CDC says Americans should get each week. Today I feel better, have greater strength and endurance than I had in my twenties, and I can keep up with my wife and daughter wherever they want to walk.

I wrote this book recognizing that most Christians struggle to pursue the simple spiritual exercises needed to have a healthy spiritual life; the kind of things that lead us to a fulfilling and fruitful walk with Christ.

Because we're a bit out of shape, we can't keep up when Jesus calls us to follow. We can't or don't do the things he would have us do, often failing to even realize he's asking. Instead of the peace that passes all understanding we only know anxiety and stress. And in our weakened state, it's easy to succumb to temptation or to fall away from our faith altogether.

St. Paul notes, "Train yourself for a holy life! While physical training has some value, training in holy living is useful for everything. It has promise for this life now and the life to come" (1 Timothy 4:7b-8). Paul regularly used the analogy of physical training to describe the Christian life.

As with physical exercise, the spiritual exercises are not rocket science. They are simple practices that anyone can do. I've focused on five essential practices in this book, and looked at how we pursue them on our own and in community. As with physical exercise, there are hundreds, perhaps thousands, of things you could do to train spiritually, but these are five essentials taught or modeled through the Bible. Once again they are,

- Worship (including prayer),
- Study (listening for God including reading Scripture),

- Serve (acts of kindness),
- Give (generosity toward God and others),
- Share (witnessing to your faith).

Worship, Study, Serve, Give and Share. With each, I challenged you to a simple, achievable, measurable, and specific goal using your fingers to remember. Measurable goals increase the likelihood that we'll pursue the exercises. Paul notes, "This is how I run—not without a clear goal in sight" (1 Corinthians 9:26). Here are the goals I encouraged you to set for pursuing these practices on your own and with others through your church:

- Pray five times a day and worship weekly.
- Read five verses of the Bible daily and study the Bible in a small group.
- Practice five acts of intentional kindness a week and serve with others.
- Extend five acts of generosity toward others each month, and give generously to God through the church.
- Let others know you are a Christian and invite five people to church each year.

The important thing is not the specific numbers. In most cases, these are simply beginning points, like my seven-minute workout. You may need to start with lower goals, or you may already be surpassing some of these. Ultimately, I hope you exceed all of these challenge goals. The point is not the numbers, the point is spiritual maturity, loving God with all your heart, soul, mind, and strength, loving your neighbor as you love yourself, and walking with Jesus wherever he leads. The challenge goals and the five practices are a means to that end.

I want to end by inviting you to imagine what would happen if your church decided to make these practices a part of the goals for every member as we are striving to do at Church of the Resurrection. The average church in America has an attendance of around 50 people. If an average church were to take this challenge, lifting up these expectations for each member, a congregation of just 50 people will have, over the course of one year,

- Prayed, giving thanks 91,250 times
- Studied 91,250 verses of Scripture
- Committed 13,000 acts of kindness
- Shared 3,000 acts of extraordinary generosity
- Invited 250 people to worship[1]

Can we really get every member of a church to do all of these things? Perhaps not, but I suspect many would accept the challenge. At Church of the Resurrection, after preaching an initial Lenten sermon series on the five essential practices (a series upon which this book is based), we made an intentional commitment to teaching and reinforcing these practices each year for the next decade. I'm including references to them in our sermons, we're designing our discipleship programming around them, and these are, and have been for some time, our five expectations of membership that we share with all new members. My hope is that a significant number of our members will make these practices holy habits in their lives. But that has to start with me and our leaders in the church.

But is all this talk about numbers really necessary? Let's just have the practices without the numbers. Practices without numbers and goals become good intentions. But setting goals, even small ones, and accomplishing them, stretches us, motivates us, and pushes us to do more than we otherwise would do.

I have a smart watch I wear when I exercise. This morning I walked 3.4 miles in just over forty minutes—about twelve minutes a mile. My watch told me I burned 460 calories and that this was my eighth fastest walk of the last year. Why does my watch tell me this? Because numeric goals and measurements stretch, motivate, and push us to do more than we otherwise would have done. Without my goal to walk three miles, or to walk forty minutes, I might not have walked at all today, or if I did, I'd have stopped after the first mile.

Each of the goals associated with the Five Essential Practices is simply a measurable starting point that I hope might challenge and stretch you, and perhaps your church, as you seek to walk with Christ. And in sharing the potential impact of an entire congregation pursuing these goals, I hoped to give a vision of the kind of collective impact these goals could have on your congregation, its community, and the world.

Jesus calls you to follow him, to walk with him, and he promises to walk with you. Are you ready?

NOTES

Chapter 1

1. Janice Kaplan, "Gratitude Survey," Penn, Schoen, Berland, June–October 2012, 2, accessed August 5, 2019, available from https://www.google.com/url ?sa=t&rct=j&q=&esrc=s&source=web&cd=2&ved =2ahUKEwjYqZy68rXkAhVtm-AKHeItAPIQFjABegQ IBBAC&url=https%3A%2F%2Fgreatergood.berkeley .edu%2Fimages%2Fuploads%2FJTF_GRATITUDE _REPORTpub.doc&usg=AOvVaw0bOLBnofdRNOR GT3h1CzA6.

2. David Steindl-Rast, "Want to be happy? Be grateful," TED.com video, 14:19, June 2013, accessed August 5, 2019, https://www.ted.com/talks/david_steindl _rast_want_to_be_happy_be_grateful.

3. Mikaela Conley, "Thankfulness Linked to Positive Changes in Brain and Body," ABC News, November 23, 2011, accessed August 29, 2019, https://abcnews .go.com/Health/science-thankfulness/story?id =15008148.

4. Paul J. Mills et al., "The Role of Gratitude in Spiritual Well-Being in Asymptomatic Heart Failure Patients," Spirituality in Clinical Practice 2, no. 1 (2015): 5–17, accessed August 29, 2019, http://35s3f14rw1s1sr3rc1nk656ib9-wpengine .netdna-ssl.com/wp-content/uploads/2015/10 /SCP-Artcile.pdf.

5. "Gratitude Study," The Chopra Foundation, accessed August 9, 2019, https://www.choprafoundation.org /education-research/past-studies/gratitude-study/.

6. Ocean Robbins, "The Neuroscience of Why Gratitude Makes Us Healthier," *Huffington Post*, November 4, 2011, accessed August 29, 2019, https://www.huffingtonpost.com/ocean-robbins /having-gratitude-_b_1073105.html.

Chapter 2

1. "Americans are Fond of the Bible, Don't Actually Read It" LifeWay Research, April 25, 2017. https://lifewayresearch.com/2017/04/25/lifeway -research-americans-are-fond-of-the-bible-dont -actually-read-it/.

Chapter 3

1. To find out more about the church's Beds Ministry visit: https://cor.org/leawood/search?q=beds+ministry #d/serve/4588/cor_l.

2. Martin Luther King Jr., "A Knock at Midnight," (speech, Mt. Zion Baptist Church, Cincinnati, Ohio, June 5, 1963). https://kinginstitute.stanford.edu /king-papers/documents/knock-midnight.

3. "7 Scientific Benefits of Helping Others," http:// mentalfloss.com/article/71964/7-scientific-benefits -helping-others.

4. "Good Giving: Why Helping Others Is Good for Your Heart and Your Health," https://healthplans .providence.org/fittogether/find-your-fit/emotional -well-being/self-care-caring-for-others/good-giving/.

5. For those who may be curious, the other two rules are "doing no harm..." and "attending upon the ordinances of God."

Chapter 4

1. Viktor Frankl, *Man's Search for Meaning*, trans. Ilse Lasch (Boston: Beacon Press, 2006), 37.

2. Among others, this is a summary of two studies: https://www.forbes.com/sites/daviddisalvo/2018 /09/10/generosity-isnt-just-about-doing-good-its -also-good-for-our-mental-health-suggests-new -study/#7cae548d5286.

3. "The Other Christmas Gift," UPtv, published December 15, 2015, accessed September 3, 2019, https://www.youtube.com/watch?v=OnZfRh _7tzw&feature=youtu.be.

Chapter 5

1. Usually attributed to St. Francis of Assisi, but there is some debate as to whether he said this or not.

Chapter 6

1. We require persons to commit to pursuing all five practices, but we don't require adherence to all of the challenges within each practice—one could

join, for instance, and not pray five times a day, but not without committing to grow in the practice of prayer. A person can join without committing to tithing, or five acts of generosity, but all must return an annual stewardship commitment card and set a goal of growing in generosity.

2. These are just part of the membership vows of The United Methodist Church. I've appreciated this list of practices, but it is a bit vague and difficult to measure. The five essential practices are an attempt to make them specific and measurable. "Presence" in the UM membership vows seems to mean attendance in worship and programs, though this is never explicitly said. Our Five Essential Practices tie worship and prayer together in the first practice, and explicitly mention Scripture study both in small groups and individually in the second practice. Aside from this the Five Practices put service before giving, while the UM vows place giving before service.

3. For a more detailed account of the final twenty-four hours of Jesus' life or the final words of Jesus from the cross, see my books *24 Hours That Changed the World* (Nashville: Abingdon Press, 2009) and *Final Words from the Cross* (Nashville: Abingdon, 2011).

4. John frequently uses seemingly mundane details as clues hoping the reader will look deeper. For other examples see my book *John: The Gospel of Light and Life* (Nashville: Abingdon, 2015).

5. William Willimon, *Thank God It's Friday: Encountering the Seven Last Words from the Cross* (Nashville: Abingdon Press), 6.

6. Isaac Watts, 1707, "When I Survey the Wondrous Cross," *The United Methodist Hymnal* (Nashville, TN: The United Methodist Publishing House, 1989), 298.

Postscript

1. To determine what these numbers would look like in your congregation, multiply average worship attendance times 1,825 to calculate how many prayers and verses of Scripture your congregation will have prayed or studied. To determine the number of acts of kindness multiply average worship attendance times 260 for the total number of acts of kindness you will have pursued together. To determine the number of people your congregation will have invited multiply average weekly attendance times 5.

ACKNOWLEDGMENTS

I am profoundly grateful for the people of The United Methodist Church of the Resurrection with whom I have walked on this journey of faith the last twenty-nine years. The lessons and practices in this book have been tested and lived not only in my life but in theirs.

I also want to recognize our lay and staff leadership who served on the church's 2030 Vision Team. In 2018, we embarked on a journey to discern where God was leading our congregation and what God was asking of our church over the ensuing twelve years. This was an amazing team who prayed and contemplated God's will for our congregation for the next decade and beyond. With the help of Will Mancini and Clint Grider of Auxano, the consultants who led us in this discernment process, we were moved to place an increasing focus on the five essential practices that had formed the core of our membership expectations and discipleship path for the last twenty-nine years and to look for ways to share these with other congregations so that we, and others, might "close the gap" between the Christians we are and the Christians God calls us to be.

I want to thank my colleagues at Abingdon Press, Susan Salley and Brian Sigmon, who were willing to dream with me about this book and then work together to strengthen the manuscript. I'm also grateful for Alan Vermilye, Tim Cobb, Leigh Ray, Pat Holland, Laura Lockhart, Tracey Craddock, and others at Abingdon, each of whom played an important part in making this book a reality. I'm also deeply indebted to the amazing team at United Methodist Communications, and those who joined me for the filming of the small group videos produced to be used alongside this book.

Finally, I want to thank my wife, LaVon, who has been my constant companion in this walk with Christ since I first met her as a cute fifteen-year-old girl in youth group. God has used her, and continues to use her, to help me walk the walk.

Adam Hamilton
Fall 2019

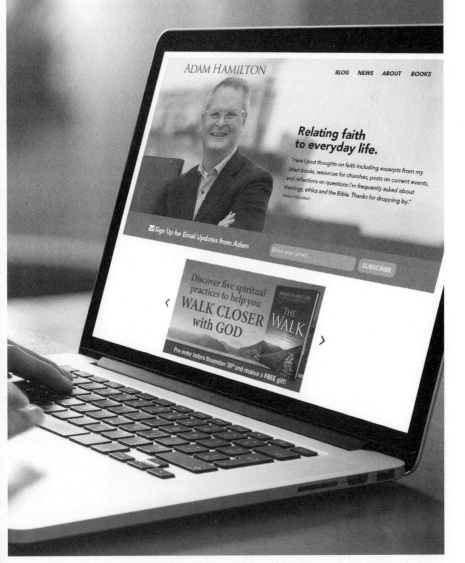